Editors: Wang Tianxing and Shi Yongnan

Translated : Liu Zongren

Texts : Shi Yongnan, Wang Tianxing, Li Yin and Wei Yuqing

Photos : Wang Tianxing, Zhu Li, Li Chungeng, Dong Zonggui, Wenfa, Wang Chunshu, He Bingfu, Hu Weibiao, Zhang Zhaoji, Liu Chungen, Jiang Jingyu

明 清 帝 后 陵

Imperial Tombs of the Ming and Qing Dynasties

中国世界语出版社 北 京

Published by China Esperanto Press, Beijing

ISBN 7-5052-0264-2/K.33

Published by China Esperanto Press, Beijing
Distributed by China Internationa! Book Trading Corporation
35 Chegongzhuang Xilu, Beijing 100044, China

P.O. Box 399, Beijing, China

Printed in the People's Republic of China

漫 话 墓 葬

　　墓葬,起源于灵魂观念的产生。灵魂,是非物质的东西,是人们幻想中寓于人身而又主宰人体的观念。灵魂观念的产生,源于远古人类对自己身体构造的无知,他们认为人的思想或感觉,不是身体内部的活动,而另有一个灵魂在支配着,精神与肉体是分开的。人体虽然离开了人世,但灵魂仍然活着,这些不死的灵魂还会回到阳间来降临祸福。因此,人们对死去的亲人不仅怀有感情上的思念,还盼望他们能够在另一世界过美好生活,并对本族本家的后人加以庇护,于是产生了埋葬死者、随葬器物的思想意识。但是,生活在"阳间"的人无法知道所谓"阴间"的情况,他们只能根据阳间的生活来设计阴间生活。所以,墓葬往往是人间生活的体现。

　　墓葬,随着社会发展而变化。大约从原始社会中期开始,人类产生了灵魂观念,便有了原始的墓葬。中国的奴隶社会进入春秋时期(前770—前476年)以后,孔子大力提倡"孝道",厚葬之风因此大盛,后经历代而不衰,并逐渐形成一套隆重复杂的祭祀礼仪和墓葬制度。于是,坟墓被认为是安葬祖宗及父母之首丘,上可尽送终之孝,下可为启后之谋。上自皇帝,下至百姓,无不对坟墓的安置特别重视。

　　帝王是中国最高的统治者,"溥天之下,莫非王土;率土之滨,莫非王臣"。故其墓葬规格与形式皆为当时最高水准。明代是中国文化史上集大成者,体现在帝王陵寝上较前代完备并形成定制。清人入关后基本继承了明代传统,不同的是,它兴起于中国东北,且为女真族(满族),故融有一些东北满族的地方特色。可以说,明清帝后陵体现着中国帝王陵寝的最高水准。

　　纵观中国历代帝王陵寝,一个显著的特点是,与山、水结下了不解之缘,其症结实则是一个"风水"问题。中国"风水术"源远流长,历代风水学家概括出一个"风水宝地"的环境模式:其北有连绵高山为屏障,南有远山近丘遥相呼应,左右两侧有低岭环护,内有广阔平原,河流穿坪蜿蜒流去。这个模式被称为"四神地"或"四灵地",是阳宅、阴宅皆追求的理想境界。

　　帝王陵寝自当选择最好的"风水宝地"。所以,历代帝王几乎均按此模式命人精心勘察,着意挑选。"万年吉地"选中以后,须按体制营建一系列建筑,其总体布局与皇宫无异,大体为"前朝后寝"。加上前边长长的神道,形成庞大而森严的建筑群体。

　　所谓神道,系指通向祭殿和坟前的导引大道,以壮观瞻。帝陵前均有神道,但每一陵区内仅一条主神道,即首帝陵前的神道。如明十三陵以长陵为主,清东陵以孝陵为主,清西陵以泰陵为主。其余为次神道,规模较小,接在主神道上,称作"以次接主"。整个陵区由神道连接成一个整体。明清时期的帝王陵神道,可谓发展到了顶点。明十三陵神道全长 7 公里多;清东陵神道亦长达 5 公里,道旁建筑和石刻完全仿照十三陵布置,依次为石牌坊、大红门、更衣殿(祭陵时更衣之所)、神功圣德碑楼、影壁山(利用原有土丘加工堆筑成山,使人从外不能一眼望穿)、石望柱、石象生、龙凤门、七孔桥,等等。

其次为祭祀建筑区,这是陵园地面建筑主体部分,供祭祀之用。主要建筑为祭殿,祭殿旁有配殿、廊庑;前有焚帛炉、大门等,后有祭坛。如清西陵,其祭祀建筑大致为:神道碑亭、神厨库、朝房(祭祀时烧制奶茶、制做面食的地方)、值房(守陵人住宿之处)、隆恩门、焚帛炉、东西配殿、隆恩殿、三孔桥、陵寝门、二柱门、石五供等。

再就是封土,即坟上之土堆。中国帝王陵寝封土经过了"方上"、"以山为陵"两个阶段,至明清采用"宝城宝顶"形式。其建筑方法是在地宫上砌筑高大的砖城,城内填土,使之高出城墙形成一圆顶。城墙上设垛口和女墙,宛如一座小城。这城墙称为"宝城",高出的圆顶曰"宝顶"。宝城有圆形、长圆形两种。明陵多是圆形,清陵则多为长圆形。宝城前尚有一突出的方形城台,上建明楼,称之为"方城明楼",楼内竖立皇帝或皇后的谥号碑,作为某一帝王陵的标志。如明十三陵中长陵明楼内有"大明成祖文皇帝之陵"的朱砂石碑。方城明楼与宝城宝顶是结合为一体的建筑,有两种上下城墙的方式:一是从方城外侧两旁上下;一是从方城正中开券洞,进洞后有一哑吧院,又名月牙城,然后从此城两侧上下。个别方城仅有券洞,无哑巴院,人从券洞两侧支券登城,如泰东陵即如此,这是特例。

宝城宝顶和方城明楼构成的坟头,突出地显示了陵寝的庄严气氛,也增强了建筑的艺术效果。

最后是地下宫殿。地宫是帝王陵寝的重要部分,又叫"玄宫"、"幽宫"等,因其结构豪华富丽,堪与帝王的人间宫殿媲美,俗称地下宫殿。由于地宫是埋葬帝王身骨和殉葬大量珍品之处,过去不为世人所知,所以一直是个谜。自科学地发掘了明十三陵定陵地宫后,才解开了这个千古之谜。

定陵地宫位于宝顶之下,距宝顶 27 米,总面积 1195 平方米,平面布局仍采用"前朝后寝"之制,极力模仿死者生前的生活方式,以追求"死犹如生"的境界。地宫前半部为一长而宽的隧道,作为进入地宫的前奏,犹如紫禁城前的重门广道。宫内分前、中、后三殿及左、右两配殿,殿与殿之间均设门、道予以区隔。前殿之前,尚有一方形券室作为前廷,象征紫禁城前广场。前殿也是作为前导建筑。中殿才是所谓"前朝"部分,殿内摆放三个汉白玉石雕造的宝座,正中一个是万历皇帝朱翊钧的主位,其前已非群臣朝拜的热闹场面,而是摆放着琉璃"五供"和大龙缸长明灯。后殿是地宫主要部分,规模最大,高9.5米,长30.1米,宽9.1米,即所谓"后寝"。万历皇帝的棺椁陈放于棺床正中,孝端、孝靖两皇后棺木置于两旁,周围陈列着玉料、梅瓶及满装珍贵殉葬品的红漆大木箱。箱内金银器物、珠宝玉石、日用物品应有尽有,可谓帝后所用均从人间带到了地府。

特别值得一提的是帝后陵的殉葬。殉葬的本意大约有两点:一是作为纪念性,表达生者感情上对死者的怀念;二是灵魂观念所引起的,认为人死后到另一个世界去,仍过着同人世间一样的生活,也需要生产工具、日用品和爱好的玩物。为了使死者在"阴间"过得如同"阳间"一样美好,便用殉葬的方式把这些东西送给他们。殉葬中最残忍的当首推"人殉"。在奴隶社会,奴隶是奴隶主的私有财产,可以任意转卖、赠送、宰杀。一批批奴隶被活埋或杀死,作为墓主人的殉葬品被埋进墓室。到奴隶社会后期,一些奴隶主大概感到用大量奴隶殉葬未免耗费生产力,损失太大,便想出用"俑"代替活人殉葬。秦始皇兵马俑便是一个俑殉奇迹,其数量之多,体形之雄大,制作之精美,不仅是空前的,亦可能是绝后的。

但是,帝王驾崩,时有圈定妃嫔殉葬之事发生。明十三陵中,长、献、景三陵就有人殉葬,殉葬者不入地宫而入"井"。陵区东西二井葬朱棣妃十六人。这些赐死的随葬宫妃,是皇帝的地下随侍,虽赐死却无资格入地宫,埋葬她们的坟因竖葬而称为"井"。

由于中国数千年奉行"厚葬",历代统治阶级均把大量财富埋进坟墓。除金银财宝外,还有数量可观的日用器物、工艺美术品、文房四宝、图书绘画以及生产工具和科技成果等,无所不有,无所不包,称得上是一座座地下宝库。

墓葬因蒙昧无知而产生,又因盲目信崇而发展,至封建社会后期臻于完美。仙去的人原本幻想在"阴间"继续享受"阳间"的美好生活,殊不知,这却给今人留下了丰富的历史文化遗产。优美的环境,精美的建筑,珍贵的文物,完备的体制,无一不为我们认识过往的历史提供了宝贵的实物佐证。

Burial History in China

Ancient people had no anatomical knowledge. They believed that thinking and feelings were dominated by something outside the physical body which they called "soul". When people died their souls remained alive that would still manipulate people's life. So they buried their dead except for old memory's sake they wished the dead would lead a good life in the netherworld and bring good fortunes to the living ones. Since the living ones were unable to know what the netherworld was like they prepared the life of their dead in there as if they were still living: they buried with the dead objects they would need and designed the burial ground like a living place.

The burial ways kept changing as the society advanced. The concept of soul appeared in the middle of the primitive society and the people began to bury their dead at that time. During the Spring and Autumn Period (770-476 B.C.) in the late slave society the burial ceremony was greatly elaborated due to the doctrine of filial piety advocated by Confucius. A grand, complex set of sacrificial and worshipping rites was gradually formed during the following feudal empires. The burial ground was regarded as an ancestral shrine and highly respected by both the common people and rulers.

Kings and emperors held the highest power — "All the land under heaven belongs to the king; all the people on the earth are subjects of the king" — as the saying goes. So the burial grounds of emperors in China were the grandest in design and scale. The Chinese feudal culture came to its zenith during the Ming Dynasty (1368-1644). The imperial burial grounds of that period became the most extravagant in Chinese history. The rulers of the Qing Dynasty (1644-1911) were nomadic Manchus from Northeast China. They inherited the traditions of the Ming Dynasty, but kept some of their original customs. Their burial grounds followed those of the Ming rulers.

The imperial burial grounds are closely related to the surrounding landscape. The practice of geomancy appeared very early in China. Geomancers developed a concept for an ideal residence for both the living and the dead: mountains to the near north as a shelter, mountains to the far south as a response to the mountains in the north, low hills on the right and left sides as guards, broad flat land on the site, and rivers flowing nearby. Such a place was called "land of four divinities" or "land of four spirits".

The location of an imperial burial ground was always the best spot. Geomancers were sent to conduct careful surveys of the site. As the site was decided upon, a series of structures would be erected. They would be arranged as those in the imperial palace: with an outer court for the emperor to handle state affairs and an inner court as living quarters. A long path called "Sacred Way" led to the entrance of the tomb.

A main Sacred Way to the head tomb (the oldest) and subsidiary Sacred Ways to lesser tombs are always found in an imperial cemetery. The head tomb of the thirteen

Ming Tombs is Changling, the head tomb of the Eastern Qing Tombs is Xiaoling and the head tomb of the Western Qing Tombs is Tailing. The subsidiary Sacred Ways are connected to the main Sacred Way. The Sacred Ways of the Ming Tombs are seven kilometers long and those of the Eastern Qing Tombs are five kilometers long. Along the Sacred Ways are a stone archway, Grand Palace Gate, the Hall for Changing Clothes, Divine Merits Stele Tower, Screen Hill (an earth mound to block direct view to the tomb), Stone columns, stone sculptures, the Dragon-Phoenix Gate and Seven-Arch Bridge.

The buildings at the end of a Sacred Way are for sacrificial ceremonies. The main hall is flanked by smaller halls and corridors. In front of the main hall is a burner and the front gate; behind it is a sacrificial altar. The ceremonial structures in the Western Qing Tombs are arranged in this order: Stele Pavilion on the Sacred Way, Kitchen Storehouse, Pastry Room, Guardhouse, Long'en Gate, Sacrificial Paper Burner, Wing Halls on the east and west, Long'en Hall, Three-Arch Bridge, Gate to the Burial Mound, Double-Pillar Gate and the Five Stone Altar Pieces.

After the burial chamber was completed, a high and thick wall was built to go around the chamber that went up higher than the ground level, then earth was piled inside the wall to form a mound with its top higher than the wall. The wall-enclosed area is called the "Precious Citadel" and the mound is called the "Precious Top". The high wall is complete with battlements and crenels. The layout of the walls is either round or rectangular. Most walls of the Ming Tombs are round, and most of the Qing Tombs are rectangular. There is a square walled area in front of each tomb called "Square City". A tower on top of it houses a stone tablet inscribed with the dead emperor's posthumous title in crimson color. The tower can be reached by two ramps either inside the wall or outside the wall. An arched passageway in the Square City leads to the earth mound. Some tombs have a courtyard inside the wall; some do not.

The high earth mound and the tower on top of the Square City greatly enhance the solemnity and grandeur of the imperial burial ground.

The mammoth burial chamber, called "Underground Palace", is matchable to the palaces for the living emperors for its extravagant design and decoration. Many precious objects were buried along with the dead emperor. Since the imperial tombs were heavily guarded they had remained mysterious to the common people until Dingling of the Ming Tombs was excavated in 1956.

The Underground Palace of Dingling is 27 meters directly below the surface. The 1,195-square-meter ground is composed of an "Outer Court" and an "Inner Court" like the imperial palace. A wide, long tunnel leads to the three main vaults along a central axis: the Ante-Chamber, the Sacrificial Chamber with annexes on each side, and the Burial Chamber itself. Gates and passageways link up the vaults. A square area with an arched ceiling symbolizes the front court of the Hall of Supreme Harmony in the imperial palace. Behind the Ante-Chamber is the Sacrificial Chamber, which serves as the Outer Court. There are three white marble thrones in the center of this hall. The central throne was for Emperor Wan Li (Zhu Lijun). In front of each throne is a set of five altar-pieces made of glazed pottery and a huge porcelain jar still containing oil and wick that were supposed to burn and provide "everlasting light". The Burial Chamber, the main part of the Underground Palace and the largest vault in it, is 9.5 meters high, 30.1 meters long and 9.1 meters wide. The coffin of Emperor Wan Li is placed in the middle. On either side of it are the coffins of his empresses Xiaoduan and Xiaojing. On either side to the left and right of the coffins were jade pieces, vases and red-lacquered wooden chests that contained precious stones, ornamental articles of gold, silver, pearls and every kind of daily necessities.

People in ancient times believed that the dead would lead a life much similar to that of the living. They would need production implements, articles for daily use and things for entertainment. So these things were buried along with the dead. The most cruel offering was human lives. In the slave society, slaves were private property of their owners. They were sold, given away as presents or killed at will. Many slaves were killed or buried alive as offerings to their dead owners. In the late period of the slave society, however, the owners made pottery human figures as offerings for they thought to kill slaves was too much a cost of their production forces. The life-size terra-cotta human figuers excavated at the tomb of Emperor Qin Shi Huang are such an example. The workmanship of these pottery sculptures is the best so far found in China.

But some emperors still wanted their favorite concubines to go with them to the netherworld. Human offerings were found at Changling, Xianling and Jingling of the Ming Tombs. But the human sacrifices were not in the main burial vaults but in "wells" nearby. They were buried alive in a standing posture, still waiting on the dead emperor. Sixteen imperial concubines of Emperor Zhu Di, five of Emperor Zhu Gaochi and ten of Emperor Zhu Zhanji were buried alive in this manner.

Royal family members, the rich and high-ranking officials in the feudal society through several thousand years took numerous articles of daily use, arts and crafts, jewelries, books, paintings, tools for writing and even results of scientific research with them to their burial grounds. Every large tomb is an underground treasurehouse. They are today valuable materials for the study of Chinese history and precious cultural relics for people to admire.

目 录
CONTENTS

明 帝 后 陵

　　明朝是中国封建社会后期一个很重要的历史阶段,共历十六帝,统治中国二百七十七年。开国皇帝朱元璋,出身贫寒,曾削发为僧,后参加元末农民起义军"红巾军",并逐渐成为起义军领袖,在统一江南大片疆土的基础上,于1368年在应天府(今江苏省南京市)即位称帝,建国号大明。朱元璋在位三十一年,病逝于南京,葬于东郊,是为孝陵。

　　朱元璋逝后,因其长子早亡,传位皇长孙朱允炆,即建文帝。新帝为加强中央集权,采纳朝中大臣建议,实行"削藩"政策。此举触犯了分封诸王,实力最强的燕王朱棣(藩邸在北京)以"清君侧"为辞,于1399年发动了历时四年的"靖难之役",攻陷南京,夺取帝位,翌年改元永乐。建文帝不知所终,故无陵寝。

　　永乐帝留恋其兴王之地——北平府,故于永乐四年(1406年)征调工匠、民夫上百万人,开始修建北京。永乐五年,皇后徐氏去世,朱棣未在南京建陵,却在北京昌平选定陵址,历时八年修成长陵。此后,嗣皇帝又在其左右相继建陵,直至1644年末帝思宗朱由检葬入田贵妃坟园,在北京先后共建有十四座明代帝后合葬陵。其中景帝陵建于京西金山之原,其余十三座陵寝均在京郊昌平县境内,故称"明十三陵"。

　　明十三陵距北京约50公里,陵区以永乐帝长陵所在的天寿山为主峰,东西北三面群山环抱,宛如一座天然大庭院,院门南开,蟒山、虎山雄居两侧,恰似一龙一虎镇守大门。向南是宽阔的盆地,温榆河从西北蜿蜒流来。整个陵区方圆40公里,十三位皇帝、二十三位皇后以及众多的妃嫔、太子、公主、从葬宫女等长眠在这松柏掩映的重山叠峦之中。

　　明帝陵一改历代墓冢覆斗形的建筑格局,整体平面呈前方后圆,具有"前殿后宫"的寓意。其规模宏大,布局严谨,俨然是紫禁城在另一世界的翻版。

Imperial Tombs of the Ming Dynasty

Sixteen emperors ruled the Ming Dynasty from 1368 to 1644 over 277 years. Zhu Yuanzhang, the founder, came from a poor peasant family. Once a Buddhist monk, he joined the Red Turban peasant army who was fighting against the Yuan court and eventually rose to become its chief leader. In 1368, after having taken over the vast areas south of the Yangtze River, Zhu Yuanzhang established the Ming Dynasty with its capital in Yingtianfu (today Nanjing, Jiangsu Province). He died after 31 years on the throne and was buried in the eastern suburbs of the capital. His tomb is Xiaoling.

Zhu Yuanzhang's eldest son died young. His eldest grandson Zhu Yunwen took over the reign to become Emperor Jian Wen. He adopted the proposal of court officials to reduce the power of regional garrison commanders who were the many sons of Zhu Yuanzhang. Zhu Di, Prince of Yan (with headquarters in Beijing), was enraged and launched an expedition to the capital in 1399. He usurped the throne in four years and became Emperor Yong Le. The dethroned emperor disappeared with no one knew where. So there is no tomb for him.

In 1406 Emperor Yong Le conscripted over one million workers to renovate Beijing. When Empress Xu died in 1407 he decided to bury her in Beijing instead in the former capital Nanjing, where his father's tomb was located. The new imperial cemetery was in Changping County north to Beijing city. The tomb for Empress Xu was finished in four years. Emperor Yong Le was buried in the same tomb when he died. The following emperors of the Ming Dynasty also built their tombs near Changling, the tomb of Emperor Yong Le and his empresses. In 1644, Zhu Youjian, the last emperor of the Ming Dynasty, hanged himself when a peasant army took over Beijing. He was buried in the tomb of Lady Tian, one of his concubines. The Ming court built 14 tombs near Beijing city. But the tomb of Emperor Jing Di is located at Jinshan Mountain in the western outskirts of Beijing. There are 13 tombs in Changping County, commonly known today as the "Thirteen Ming Tombs".

The Ming Tombs are 50 kilometers northwest from Beijing proper. Tianshou Mountain where the tomb of Emperor Yong Le is located is the main peak. Mountain peaks to its east, west and north form a semicircle with a flat basin inside. Mangshan and Hushan mountains to the south stand like two guards at the front gate. Further south is a broad flat plain. The Wenyu River flows by from the northwest. The entire cemetery, 40 kilometers around, keeps the remains of 13 emperors, 23 empresses and many imperial concubines, princes and princesses.

Tombs before the Ming Dynasty were ususally round earth mounds. The layout of the Ming Tombs is square in front and round behind, symbolizing the "front court for official matters and rear palace as living quarters" in the imperial palace. The layout and design of the imperial burial complex are also as grand and meticulous as that of the imperial palace.

Xiaoling   The burial ground of Zhu Yuanzhang (reigned between 1368 and 1398), founder of the Ming Dynasty, is located at the southern side of Zijin Mountain in the eastern suburbs of Nanjing. Construction of the tomb began in 1376 and was finished in seven years. Along the central axis there are Divine Merit Stele Tower, stone sculptures, the Sacred Way Stele Pavilion, Offerings Hall, "Square City" with Memorial Tower and the walled earth mound. The following Ming emperors all built their tombs in this pattern.

孝陵   明朝开国皇帝朱元璋(1368－1398年在位)陵寝,位于南京市东郊紫金山南麓的独龙阜。洪武九年(1376年)开始营建,历时七年完工。中轴线上主体建筑有:神功圣德碑楼、石象生、神道碑亭、享殿、方城明楼、宝城宝顶等,开创了明代陵寝的规制。

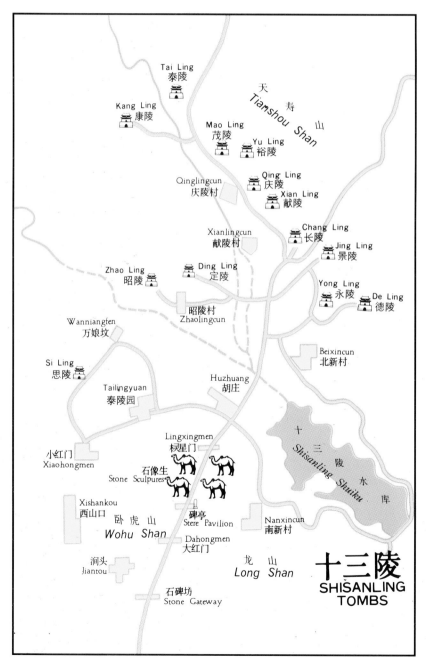

Tai Ling
泰陵

Kang Ling
康陵

Mao Ling
茂陵

Yu Ling
裕陵

天　寿　山
Tianshou Shan

Qinglingcun
庆陵村

Qing Ling
庆陵

Xian Ling
献陵

Xianlingcun
献陵村

Chang Ling
长陵

Jing Ling
景陵

Zhao Ling
昭陵

Ding Ling
定陵

Yong Ling
永陵

De Ling
德陵

昭陵村
Zhaolingcun

Wanniangfen
万娘坟

Beixincun
北新村

Si Ling
思陵

Tailingyuan
泰陵园

Huzhuang
胡庄

Lingxingmen
棂星门

十
三
陵
水
库
Shisanling Shuiku

小红门
Xiaohongmen

石像生
Stone Sculpures

Xishankou
西山口

卧 虎 山
Wohu Shan

碑亭
Stere Pavilion

Nanxincun
南新村

Dahongmen
大红门

涧头
Jiantou

龙 山
Long Shan

十三陵
SHISANLING
TOMBS

石碑坊
Stone Gateway

雪映帝陵 明十三陵位于北京西北郊昌平县,陵区面积达 40 平方公里,东、西、北三面群山耸立,如障似屏,雄伟壮观。陵区有一条规整的中轴线,依次建有石牌坊、大宫门、大碑楼、石象生、龙凤门等建筑,是明朝陵寝制度的完美体现。

Ming Tombs in Snow The thirteen Ming Tombs in Changping County northwest of Beijing proper occupies 40 square kilometers and are surrounded by mountains on the east, west and north. Along the central axis there are a stone archway, Grand Palace Gate, Stele Tower, stone sculptures and the Dragon-Phoenix Gate.

牌坊 又名牌楼，为门洞式纪念性建筑物，多建于庙宇、陵墓、祠堂、衙署、园林前或街道路口，用以宣扬封建礼教，标榜功德。图中牌坊为石质，是陵区最南端建筑。

Stone Archway A memorial archway is often found in temples, cemeteries, ancestral shrines, government offices, gardens and streets. It was erected to promote feudal virtues or served as a symbol of meritorious deeds. The stone archway in the picture is the southernmost structure in the Ming Tombs.

大宫门 陵区正门，旁连 40 公里围墙，为皇帝谒陵、梓宫发引的必经之路。

Grand Palace Gate There used to be a 40-kilometer-long wall stretching out from this gate to surround the cemetery. Living emperors who went to pay respect to their ancestors or dead emperors who were to be buried in the cemetery all passed through this gate.

下马碑 大宫门前东西两侧,各有石碑一通,前后两面均镌刻"官员人等至此下马"八个大字。上自皇帝,下至臣民,至此均须下马落轿,徒步进入陵区,以示对死者的尊崇。

Dismounting Tablets Two stone tablets are placed on either side of the Grand Palace Gate. Each is inscribed on both sides with "Dismount". The emperor and court officials had to get off from their horses or palanquins at this spot.

碑楼 即长陵神功圣德碑亭,始建于宣德十年(1435年)。重檐歇山四出陛,四角不远处各竖汉白玉石华表一座,如辰星拱卫,庄重肃穆。

Stele Tower The structure with multiple eaves and a gabled roof at Changling was built in 1435. Four white marble columns stand on each corner near the tower, enhancing the solemnity of the place.

神功圣德碑 为龙首龟趺石碑，通高7.91米，碑额篆刻"大明长陵神功圣德碑"。碑身正面镌文三千余字，系仁宗皇帝御笔，记述其父皇永乐帝靖难兴师、迁都北京、亲征漠北等业绩。碑阴及两侧刻有清乾隆皇帝（1735—1795年在位）、嘉庆皇帝（1796—1820年在位）谒十三陵之御笔诗文。

Divine Merit Stele   The 7. 91-meter-high stone stele sits on a giant turtle inscribed with the words: "Divine Merit Stele of Changling of the Great Ming". An inscription of 3,000 Chinese characters in the handwriting of Emperor Ren Zong on the front side of the stele records Emperor Yong Le's expedition to Nanjing, move of the capital from Nanjing to Beijing, and his battles in the desert north of the Great Wall. The inscriptions on the back side were written by Emperor Qian Long (1735-1795) and Emperor Jia Qing (1796-1820), both of the Qing Dynasty, to record their visits to the Ming Tombs.

石象生 为一组石人石兽雕刻。帝陵前设石象生,始于秦(前221－前206年)、汉(前206－220年),用以表饰坟垅,象征死者生前仪卫。十三陵石象生,依次为狮子、獬豸、骆驼、象、麒麟、马、武臣、文臣、勋臣,卧立各一对,它们是明代石雕艺术的精品。

Stone Sculptures   The custom to place stone sculptures in imperial cemeteries began in the Qin Dynasty (221-206 B. C.) and the Han Dynasty (206 B.C.-A. D. 220) to serve as ceremonial guards. Stone sculptures in the Ming Tombs include lions, xiezhi, camels, elephants, qilin unicorns, horses, and court officials. They are in pairs, one standing and one squatting. They represent the best sculpture craftsmanship of that time.

獬豸　中国古代传说中的神兽,能辨曲直,头有独角,见人相斗,以角触不直者。置于神道,以示皇帝为政清廉。

Xiezhi　The animal in Chinese mythology is said to have the power to tell right from wrong. It would use its single horn to strike at the wrong party in a fight. It was placed on the Sacred Way in the imperial cemetery as a symbol of the emperor's wise rule.

勋臣 是被皇帝赐封为公、侯、伯等爵位的大臣。石雕身着朝服,拱手持笏,是研究明代衣饰的珍贵资料。

Noble Court Officials These court officials with ranks of nobility wear ceremonial clothes and hold a tablet in cupped hands. They are valuable for the study on the clothing during the Ming Dynasty.

武臣 顶盔冠甲,手持金瓜,腰佩利剑,威武雄壮。文臣武将石雕象征皇帝拥有生死相随的忠臣良将。

Military Court Officials They wear helmets and hold a cudgel with a gold melon on top and a sword. They were supposed to protect the dead emperor as loyally as when he was alive.

龙凤门 帝后自比龙凤,他们入葬山陵必经此门,故而得名。三门额枋中央雕有石刻火焰珠,俗称火焰牌坊。

Dragon-Phoenix Gate The dragon was the symbol of the emperor and the phoenix was the symbol of the empress. After they died their coffins were carried through this gate to the tomb. Carvings in relief on top of the gate describe flames. So the gate is also called "Flame Gate".

长陵 为十三陵区第一陵,明朝第三代皇帝成祖朱棣(1402—1424 年在位)和皇后徐氏的合葬陵。陵的地面形制仿南京孝陵,中轴线上有陵门、祾恩门、祾恩殿、棂星门、方城明楼、宝城宝顶等建筑,是十三陵规模最大、体制最完整的陵寝。

Changling The head tomb of the Ming Tombs is the burial ground of Zhu Di, third emperor of the Ming Dynasty who ruled between 1402 and 1424, and his empress Xu. The layout above the ground follows that of Xiaoling in Nanjing. Structures along the central axis are the front gate to the tomb, Ling'en Gate, Ling'en Hall, Lingxing Gate, "Square City" and the wall-encircled earth mound. Changling is the largest tomb of the Ming Tombs.

陵门 单檐歇山式建筑。额枋、斗栱、檐椽均由琉璃构件拼装而成,绚丽夺目。十三陵唯长、永、定三陵建有如此规制的陵门,其他诸陵均以祾恩门代之。

Front Gate of the Tomb The brackets, beams, rafters and front board of this gate with a gabled roof are made of glazed tiles. The three gates of such making in the Ming Tombs are found at Changling, Yongling and Dingling.

鼍龙碑 位于陵门内东侧碑亭中。碑额巨龙盘绕,碑座为一鼍龙,它俗称扬子鳄,龙首龙足,遍身鳞甲,粗壮有力的背鳍直抵尾端,造型别致生动。碑身原无字,清顺治、乾隆、嘉庆三位皇帝谒陵时曾留下墨宝,镌于碑之三面。

Chinese Alligator Stele This stone stele is housed in a pavilion inside the front gate. The base is shaped like a Chinese alligator with large scales. Its powerful dorsal fin runs toward the tip of its tail. Originally there was no inscription on it. The inscriptions on three sides were written later by emperors Shun Zhi, Qian Long and Jia Qing of the Qing Dynasty.

祾恩门 单檐歇山式门楼。面阔五间,进深两间,门内匾额书有"祾恩门"三字。下承汉白玉石须弥座,装饰秀美华贵。

Ling'en Gate The gate is actually a hall with a single-eaved gabled roof and stands on a white marble terrace. A plaque bearing its name is suspended inside the gate.

焚帛炉 亦称燎炉,置于棱恩殿前左右,通体由琉璃件构成,晶莹剔透,小巧玲珑,是祭祀结束后焚烧祝版、制帛和金银锞子的窑炉。

Sacrificial Paper Burners They are two glazed pottery burners in front of Ling'en Hall. After a sacrificial ceremony the prayer paper, paper-made gold and silver ingots were burned in them.

祾恩殿内景 祾恩殿由六十根楠木巨柱支承,中间四柱最为粗壮,最高12.58米;底径达1.12米,两人环抱,不得交手。如此整材楠木柱,世所罕见。

Inside Ling'en Hall The roof of this hall is supported by 60 nanmu wood columns. The 32 columns inside the hall are 12.58 meters high. The four in the innermost are 1.12 meters in diameter. They were made out of single tree trunks, rarely seen in the world.

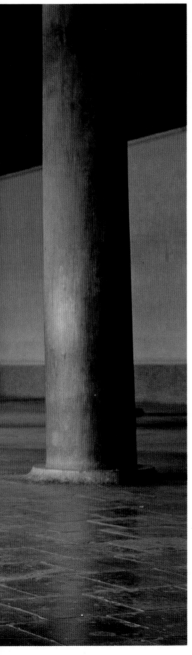

祾恩殿 亦称享殿,是放置帝王牌位和举行祭祀仪式的地方。殿内梁、柱、枋、檩均用金丝楠木作材料,不加油饰,不施彩绘,保留原木本色。此殿是中国现存最大、最壮观的楠木殿。

Ling'en Hall Also called Offerings Hall, used to keep memorial tablets with dead imperors' names. Sacrificial ceremonies were held in this hall. The beams, pillars, brackets and window frames all are made of precious nanmu wood. They are not painted as those of other buildings. This Ling'en Hall is the largest and most magnificent structure of nanmu wood extant in China.

棂星门　又称二柱门。据传源于西汉（前206—25年），初为"祈灵星，求五谷丰登"而设。门为夹山顶，隔架斗栱制作，结构复杂，精巧繁密。在由"殿"向"宫"的过渡中，起着建筑美学上的连接作用。

Lingxing Gate　Also known as "Double-Pillar Gate", the structure with a hipped roof is composed of many brackets intricately entwined. The purpose to erect such an exquisite gate was to solicit blessing from Lingxing Star for good harvests. The custom came down from the Western Han Dynasty (206 B.C.-A. D. 25).

明楼　为帝陵标志，建在圆形宝城正前方，座落于方城之上。楼上有匾额，额曰"长陵"。内有圣号碑，上刻"大明成祖文皇帝之陵"七个径尺大字。

Memorial Tower (Minglou)　The tower on top of the "Square City" in front of the earth mound is the mark of an imperial burial place. Above the gate of the tower is a plaque inscribed with the tomb's name: "Changling", and inside the tower is a stone tablet inscribed with "Tomb of Emperor Cheng Zu of the Great Ming". Each character is about 33 centimeters square.

献陵　明朝第四帝仁宗朱高炽（1424
－1425 年在位）及皇后张氏的陵寝。
仁宗即位九个月病逝，在位日浅，遗
诏其陵从俭，故十三陵中献陵最朴。

Xianling　It keeps the remains of Zhu
Gaozhi, (Ren Zong, fourth emperor of
the Qing Dynasty who ruled from 1424
to 1425), and his Empress Zhang. The
emperor died after he ascended to the
throne for only nine months. He de-
creed his burial be simple. Thus Xianling
is the simplest of the thirteen Ming
Tombs.

景陵 明朝第五帝宣宗朱瞻基（1425
－1435年在位）和继后孙氏的合葬
陵。宣宗在位十年，行仁政，予民生
息，史称仁、宣两朝的统治为"仁宣之
治"。其陵从献陵制，亦较为简朴。

Jingling It is the tomb of Zhu Zhanji
（Xuan Zong, fifth emperor of the Ming
Dynasty ruling from 1425 to 1435）and
his empress Sun. Zhu Zhanji adminis-
trated the country with benevolence and
the people lived in peace. Like Xianling
his tomb is simple.

茂陵 明朝第八位皇帝宪宗朱见深（1464－1487 年在位）和三位皇后的合葬陵寝。宪宗在位二十三年，无大作为。其陵从裕陵制，不失其豪华。但年久失修，近乎倾圮，图为明楼外景。

Maoling It is the burial ground of Zhu Jianshen (Xian Zong, eighth emperor of the Ming Dynasty who ruled from 1464 to 1487) and his three empresses. Zhu Jianshen did not do much during his 23 years of reign. His tomb followed the plan of Yuling. Though richly decorated, it fell in disrepair. The picture shows the Memorial Tower.

裕陵 位于天寿山西峰石门山南麓，是明朝第六位皇帝英宗朱祁镇（1435－1449 年和 1457－1464 年在位）之陵，皇后钱氏、周氏与其合葬。他九岁即位，重用太监王振，朝纲废弛，1449年"土木之变"中被蒙古族掳走，一年后被放回，幽居七年后发动"夺门之变"，废景泰帝，再次登上皇位，是明代唯一的两次登基的皇帝。

Yuling The tomb of Zhu Qizhen (Ying Zong, sixth emperor of the Ming Dynasty who occupied the throne twice: 1435-1449 and 1457-1464) and his empresses Qian and Zhou. He ascended to the throne at nine and took into his confidence Eunuch Wang Zhen. The court was plunged into chaos. In 1449 he was abducted by Mongols and was released one year later. After seven years living in seclusion he staged a comeback, taking the throne from Emperor Jing Tai. He was the only emperor of the Ming Dynasty who sat on the throne twice.

泰陵 明朝第九代皇帝孝宗朱祐樘
(1487—1505 年在位)和皇后张氏的
陵寝。孝宗是明代中叶少见的贤君,
他勤于理政,任用贤才,出现了"弘治
中兴"的治世局面。图为泰陵宝城围
墙。

Tailing It is the tomb of Zhu Youtang
(Xiao Zong, ninth emperor of the Ming
Dynasty who ruled between 1487 and
1505) and his empress Zhang. Zhu
Youtang was a wise and diligent ruler
who used talented officials. China became prosperous during his reign. The
picture shows the wall around the tomb.

泰陵无字碑 嘉靖十五年（1536年）增建。此前所建七陵仅长陵有神功圣德碑。世宗皇帝朱厚熜认为无碑无以彰其先祖功德，下令增建。历时四年完工。无奈此间皇上沉缅于炼丹服石，且不久即发生谋杀皇帝未遂的"壬寅宫变"，撰写碑文之事遂不了了之。此后建陵因循先例，均为无字碑。

Stele with No Inscription at Tailing The stele was added to Tailing in 1536. Before that only Changling of the seven tombs that had been built had a "Divine Merit Stele". Zhu Houcong (Emperor Shi Zong) ordered to erect a stele at Tailing as a tribute to his dead father. The project was finished in four years. Meanwhile Zhu Houcong spent most of the time on making elixir of life. Some officials plotted against his life but failed. The emperor was no more interested in writing an inscription for the stele. Later emperors of the Ming Dynasty followed his example and erected memorial steles at their tombs without an inscription.

康陵 为明朝第十代皇帝武宗朱厚照（1505－1521 年在位）和皇后夏氏陵寝。武宗，十六岁继皇帝位，养狗驯鹰，走马斗鸡，无所不能，是明代最昏庸的皇帝。康陵主要建筑无存，仅无字碑尚完好。

Kangling It is the tomb of Zhu Houzhao (Wu Zong, tenth emperor of the Ming Dynasty who ruled from 1505 to 1521) and his empress Xia. Zhu Houzhao succeeded to the throne at the age of 16 but indulged himself in a prodigal life: hunting, cockfight and horse race. He was the most fatuous ruler of the Ming Dynasty. The structures above the ground at Kangling had long collapsed except the memorial stele without an inscription.

永陵 是明朝第十一位皇帝世宗朱厚熜（1521－1566 年在位）及三位皇后的合葬陵寝。朱厚熜十五岁时由湖北兴王府接入宫中，以旁系宗支继位称帝。在位期间，兴"大礼仪之争"，杖死大臣十七人；激起宫女杨金英等发动"壬寅宫变"，是一位奢侈残暴的皇帝。永陵用料考究，规模宏阔，仅次于长陵。图为夜景——从二柱门看明楼。

Yongling It is the tomb of Zhu Houcong (Shi Zong, 11th emperor of the Ming Dynasty who ruled from 1521 to 1566) and his three empresses. He succeeded to the throne at 15 as the son of a prince whose vasalage was in present-day Hubei Province. The new emperor was cruel, beating to death 17 high-ranking officials. Yang Jinying and other palace maids tried to kill him but failed. His tomb was built with expensive materials, only less in extravagance and grandeur than Changling. The picture shows a night scene of the Memorial Tower of Yongling.

丹陛石　置于祾恩殿前御路正中，石上精刻海水江涛，云崖险峰，一龙一凤居中嬉戏。雕石构图精妙，刀法流畅，为十三陵诸多石刻中的上乘之作。

Danbi Stone Block　A stone block in front of Ling'en Hall bears exquisite relief carvings of sea and river waves, mountain peaks and a dragon and a phoenix in the middle. This one in the picture is the best of stone relief carvings in the Ming Tombs.

昭陵　为明代第十二位皇帝穆宗朱载垕(1566－1572年在位)的陵寝，孝懿、孝安、孝定三位皇后与其合葬。昭陵是十三陵中第一座被大规模修葺复原的陵墓，重修的昭陵陵制完整，建筑宏伟。

Zhaoling　The tomb keeps the remains of Zhu Zaihou (Mu Zong, 12th emperor of the Ming Dynasty ruling from 1566 to 1572) and his three empresses Xiaoyi, Xiao'an and Xiaoding. Zhaoling was the first one of the thirteen Ming Tombs being restored to its full grandeur.

皇帝腊像 朱载垕三岁被封为裕王，
十八岁成婚,同年迁出皇宫住进裕王
府,1566 年继承皇位。在位六年政绩
平平,死后葬昭陵。

Wax Figures of Emperor Mu Zong Emperor Mu Zong (Zhu Zaihou) became
the Prince of Yu at the age of three,
was married at 18 and ascended to the
throne in 1566. He was mediocre in his
six years of administration. He was
buried in Zhaoling.

昭陵宝城 为环绕宝顶封土的圆形城墙,此城较献、景等陵之宝城精致壮观。封土前部有弧形砖墙拦挡,并与方城两侧的城墙内壁相接,俗称"哑巴院"。

"Precious Citadel" of Zhaoling The wall around the earth mound of Zhaoling is more elaborately built than that of Xianling and Jingling. Another semicircle wall in front of the mound is connected with the inner side of the longer wall to form a courtyard.

定陵　明代第十三位皇帝神宗朱翊钧（1572－1620年在位）之陵，附葬孝端、孝靖两皇后，是十三陵中唯一被发掘的陵墓。朱翊钧，十岁登基，在位四十八年，是明代在位时间最长的皇帝。他二十一岁便下旨建陵，历时六年而成。此陵规制之大，用料之精，堪与永陵齐名。

Dingling　It is the burial ground of Zhu Yijun (Shen Zong, 13th emperor of the Ming Dynasty) and his empresses Xiaoduan and Xiaojing. Dingling is the only one of the Ming Tombs whose burial chamber was excavated. Zhu Yijun ascended to the throne at 10 and ruled the country for 47 years, the longest period for one emperor during the Ming Dynasty. He ordered the construction of his tomb when he was only 21. It was finished in six years. Its extravagance could be matched to that of Yongling.

定陵地宫 由前、中、后、左、右五个殿堂组成，总面积 1195 平方米。通体为砖石结构，殿顶起券，高大宽敞。

"Underground Palace" of Dingling The huge underground chamber is composed of five vaults on an area of 1,195 square meters. The spacious chamber has high arched ceilings. The whole complex is built with giant stone slabs.

地宫中殿 殿内设有三个汉白玉石雕成的宝座,用以放置帝后牌位。雕龙扶手者为皇帝宝座,雕凤扶手者为皇后宝座。座前各设一副琉璃五供和一个青花云龙大瓷缸。缸中原盛香油,放有小铜瓢和灯芯,点燃发出幽幽黄光,谓之"长明灯"。

Central Vault of the "Underground Palace" There are three white marble thrones in the central vault on which wooden tablets with the posthumous titles of the emperor and his empresses are placed. The one with carvings of dragon design on the handles belonged to the emperor and the two with carvings of phoenix design belonged to the empresses. In front of each throne is a set of alter-pieces of glazed pottery and a huge porcelain jar which contained sesame oil, a bronze dipper and wick which was supposed to provide "everlasting light".

地宫后殿 为地宫主殿。正中设棺床，上置神宗和孝端、孝靖两皇后的梓宫。棺旁摆放二十六只盛满殉葬品的红漆木箱，周围散放玉料。棺床中央有方孔，内填黄土，称"金井"，二者取义"金井玉葬"，是中国封建时代最高形式的葬礼。

Rear Vault of the "Underground Palace"
The main part of the Underground Palace keeps the confins of Emperor Shen Zong and his two empresses Xiaoduan and Xiaojing. Around the confins there are 26 red lacquered wooden chests filled with sacrificial objects and jade pieces. A square hole in the center of the dais of each coffin is filled with yellow clay which is called "Gold Well" to meet the highest requirement for burial in ancient China: "to bury the dead at the Gold Well and among jade pieces".

金冠 本名翼善冠，系明代帝王的常服冠戴。通高 24 厘米，用极细的金丝编织而成，上饰二龙戏珠，造型生动，制作精良，堪称国宝。

Gold Crown The emperors of the Ming Dynasty wore this crown with ceremonial clothes. It is 24 centimeters high and made with fine gold filaments. Two dragons play a pearl on it. The crown is a national treasure for its meticulous craftsmanship.

凤冠 皇后参加重大庆典时戴的礼服冠。冠上镶珠嵌玉，龙凤呈祥，华贵异常。定陵共出土四顶凤冠，其中一顶饰珍珠 3500 多颗，嵌宝石 150 余块。图为三龙三凤冠。

Phoenix Crown The empress put it on only at grand ceremonies. Four phoenix crowns were excavated from Dingling. The one in the picture, called "Three Dragons and Three Phoenixes Crown", is inlaid with 3,500 pearls and 150 pieces of precious stone.

衮服 皇帝在重大庆典时穿的礼服。图中衮服称为缂丝十二章衮服。缂丝,是一种通经断纬的手工丝织工艺;十二章,系指服上日、月、星辰等十二种纹饰图案。寓意皇帝代天行政,皇恩浩荡。

Ceremonial Robe This robe was used by the emperor at grand ceremonies. The cloth was specially woven. Embroidered on the robe are 12 kinds of designs such as the sun, moon and stars, meaning that the emperor ruled the land on behalf of Heaven.

玉爵杯 皇家酒器。杯的把手为一螭虎,其前爪攀附杯沿,头部隐于杯沿下,似在窥视杯中物,造型别致,妙趣横生。底座为一圆形金盘,盘中遍刻水纹,一山逢中兀出,寓意"寿山福海"。

Jade Cup This jade cup is a sacrificial object. Its handle is in the form of a dragon with its claws stretching around the cup's rim and its head looking down the inside of the cup. The cup is secured on a round base of gold bearing motifs of a mountain peak above rippling water. The meaning of the motifs is longevity and happiness.

庆陵　明朝第十四位皇帝光宗朱常
洛（1620年在位）与三位皇后的合葬
陵。光宗在位仅二十九天便崩逝，是
明朝享国最短的皇帝，其陵较为简
朴。

Qingling　　This tomb is for Zhu
Changluo (Guang Zong, 14th emperor
of the Ming Dynasty) and his three empresses. He was on the throne only for
29 days in 1620 and died, the shortest
reign during the Ming Dynasty. His
tomb is very simple.

德陵　明朝第十五位皇帝熹宗朱由校（1620－1627 年在位）之陵，皇后张氏附葬。熹宗在位七年，无大作为，其陵为死后所修，规模较小。图为神宫监大门。

Deling　This is the tomb of Zhu Youjiao (Xi Zong, 15th emperor of the Ming Dynasty who ruled between 1620 and 1627) and his empress Zhang. His tomb was built after his death. Since he had not done much in his seven years' rule, his tomb is small. The picture shows the tomb's front gate.

思陵　明朝末代皇帝思宗朱由检
（1627－1644 年在位）与周皇后和田
贵妃墓的合葬陵，在十三陵中规模
最小。思宗十七岁因"兄终弟及"即
皇帝位，尽管励精图治，但此时的明
王朝已病入膏肓，无力回天。1644
年，李自成率农民军攻入北京，思宗
自缢于煤山（即今景山）。

Siling　The tomb was built for Lady
Tian, a concubine of Zhu Youjian (the
last emperor of the Ming Dynasty whose
reign lasted from 1627 to 1644). Zhu
Youjian took over the throne at 17 after
his elder brother died. Despite his dili-
gence and high aspirations, the Ming
Dynasty kept declining. In 1644 a peasant uprising army led by Li Zicheng entered Beijing. Zhu Youjian hanged himself on a Chinese scholartree at Jingshan
behind the Imperial Palace. He and his
empress Zhou were buried in this tomb,
the smallest one of the 13 Ming Tombs.

石五供 摆放于明楼前,为象征性祭器,含香炉一只,烛台、花瓶各一对。图为思陵石五供。

Stone Altar-Pieces The five stone altar-pieces placed in front of the Memorial Tower include an incense burner, a pair of candlesticks and a pair of flower vases. These in the picture are placed at Siling.

景泰陵 位于北京近郊西山,是明朝第七代皇帝朱祁钰的陵寝,皇后汪氏附葬。朱祁钰是英宗朱祁镇的异母弟,1449年英宗被蒙古人掳走,他由监国即位称帝,随后在昌平陵区预建寿宫。七年后,英宗复辟,他被降为郕王,其陵被毁为平地。不久,朱祁钰病逝,仅以王礼葬。1475年,宪宗复其帝号,并以帝陵规制改建其陵。

Jingtailing This tomb of Zhu Qiyu, seventh emperor of the Ming Dynasty, and his empress Wang is located at the foot of the Xishan Mountains west of Beijing. Zhu Qiyu was younger brother of Emperor Ying Zong (Zhu Qizhen) of a different mother. In 1449 Emperor Ying Zong was abducted by the Mongols. Zhu Qiyu became the emperor and ordered the construction of his tomb in Changping County. Seven years later Emperor Ying Zong took over the throne and demoted Zhu Qiyu to the rank of prince. His tomb was destroyed. When he died he was buried as a prince in a tomb outside the imperial cemetery. In 1475 Emperor Xian Zong restored the title of emperor to him and renovated his tomb according to the standard for an emperor.

显陵 兴献王朱祐杬及王妃蒋氏之墓,位于湖北钟祥县。兴献王系孝宗朱祐樘异母弟,其藩邸在湖北安陆(今钟祥县),1519年病故,以王礼葬。1521年,武宗驾崩无子,朱祐杬的儿子朱厚熜得以旁系入继大统,朱祐杬亦被追封为帝,其陵按帝陵规制加以改建。神道悠悠,明楼巍巍,颇具规模。

Xianling The tomb of Zhu Youhang, Prince of Xingxian, and his wife Jiang is located in Zhongxiang County in Hubei Province. The prince was a younger brother of Emperor Xiao Zong (Zhu Youtang) of a different mother. He died in 1519. Emperor Wu Zong died childless in 1521. Zhu Houcong, a son of Zhu Youhang, became the emperor. The new emperor rebuilt his father's tomb according to the standard for an emperor.

清　帝　后　陵

　　清王朝是中国封建社会最后一个王朝,由崛起于东北的女真族创立。其奠基者清太祖努尔哈赤以"十三副遗甲"起兵,率领八旗子弟转战于白山黑水之间,临大敌不惧,受重创不馁,以勇悍立威,历三十余年征战,统一了女真族各部,于1616年在赫图阿拉(今辽宁省新宾县)建元称汗,国号大金。1618年,努尔哈赤以"七大恨"祭天,誓师征明,开始为清王朝的建立艰苦创业。1625年,大金迁都沈阳,翌年努尔哈赤疽发而逝。其子皇太极继位,是为清太宗。1635年,太宗改女真族为满族,翌年改国号为清,继续扩张疆土。1644年,清世祖顺治帝福临入关,定鼎北京,逐步统一了中国。清朝至1912年末代皇帝溥仪下诏逊位,共历十二帝,统治二百九十五年。

　　清代帝王陵寝,就其建陵年代和地理位置,可分为清初三陵、清东陵和清西陵三个陵区。

　　清初三陵即永陵、福陵、昭陵。此三陵修建时值清王朝初兴,一切典制均属草创,因而陵寝的布局和建筑形式体现了鲜明的地方特色和独特的民族风格。

　　清东陵位于河北省遵化县马兰峪境内,距北京125公里,是中国现存规模庞大、体系完整的帝后陵墓群之一。整个陵区着意于山川形势的自然美和建筑景观人文美的和谐,使其"陵制与山水相称"。它背靠层峦叠翠的昌瑞山,东依蜿蜒起伏的鹰飞倒仰山,西傍高耸入云的黄花山,南抵天然屏障金星山,更南为天台、烟墩两山对峙,形成一个险峻的陵口,名兴陵口。整个陵区之水汇集于此,形成决决大河——西大河。山映于水,水伏于山,风光绮丽,景色迷人。

　　清西陵在河北省易县境内,距北京130公里。若以北京为中心,东西二陵等距离居于两侧,构成犄角之势,而清西陵地势更佳。它北起奇峰岭,南到大燕桥,东临燕下都(公元前三世纪燕国故都之一),西至长城重要关口紫荆关,占地800多平方公里。自古就有"荆关紫气"、"拒马奔涛"、"易水寒流"等八景环绕陵区。区内陵寝背山面水,星罗棋布,规模宏大,保存完整,其间松柏青翠,杨柳依依,构成一幅绚丽多彩的画卷。

Imperial Tombs of the Qing Dynasty

The Qing Dynasty, China's last feudal empire, was founded by the Manchus from Northeast China. Nurhachi led his tiny army fighting for three decades to unify the various groups of Nüzhen tribe scattered in the Changbai Mountains and along the Heilong River. In 1616 he set up the Great Jin regime with his headquarters in today's Xinbin County, Liaoning Province. In 1618 he launched the expedition to conquer the Ming Dynasty in central China and moved his capital to Shenyang in 1625. But he died the following year. Huangtaiji, his son, took over the reins to become known in Chinese history as Emperor Tai Zong, who changed the ethnic group's name from Nüzhen to Manchu in 1635 and his regime's name from Great Jin to Qing. In 1644 Emperor Shun Zhi (Fulin) crossed the Great Wall and entered Beijing to formally set up the Qing Dynasty. The Qing Dynasty lasted for 295 years until 1912 when its last emperor Puyi abdicated. Altogether 12 emperors ruled the Qing Dynasty.

The Qing emperors are buried in three cemeteries: the Three Early Qing Tombs, Eastern Qing Tombs and Western Qing Tombs.

The Three Early Qing tombs are Yongling, Fuling and Zhaoling. Their plan and design show clear features of Northeast China and the early Manchu customs.

The Eastern Qing Tombs are located at Malanyu in Zunhua County in Hebei Province, 125 kilometers to the east of Beijing. They are one of the best preserved burial grounds in China. Its layout and buildings are well blended with the surrounding landscape. The Changrui Mountains rise behind the cemetery; the Yingfeidaoyang Mountains undulate to its east; the Huanghua Mountains rise high on its west; and the Jinxing Mountains stand on the south like a sheltering screen. Further south Tiantai Mountain and Yandun Mountain form an entrance to the cemetery which is called Xinglingkou and to which all the water in the vicinity flow to form the Xida River.

The Western Qing Tombs are located in Yixian County, Hebei Province, 130 kilometers to the west of Beijing. The imperial burial cemetery borders on Qifengling Mountain in the north, Dayan Bridge in the south, Xiadu of Yan (capital of Yan State in the third century B.C.) in the east and Zijingguan Pass of the Great Wall in the west. On this 800-square-kilometer ground there are many mountain peaks covered with ancient pine and cypress trees and rivers lined with sweeping willow trees. "Eight Natural Sights" such as "Purple Glow at Zijingguan Pass", "Turbulent Current of Juma River" and "Cold Water of Yishui River" have been known since ancient times.

清 初 三 陵

　　清初三陵又称关外三陵、盛京(今辽宁省沈阳市)三陵,为清皇室祖陵。
一处是兴京陵,顺治十六年(1659 年)改称永陵,位于赫图阿拉城启运山下苏
子河畔。一处是福陵,位于沈阳市东郊浑河北岸天柱山上,故亦称东陵。再一
处是昭陵,在沈阳市北 5 公里,亦称北陵。

　　清初三陵建于清兵入关之前,具有鲜明的地方特色和独特的民族风格。
陵区风光旖旎,古城堡式的建筑,厚重纯朴的雕刻和装饰,无不给人以神秘
静穆之感,产生怀古忆旧之情。

The Three Early Qing Tombs

　　The tombs in Shenyang, Liaoning Province keep the remains of the three earliest
rulers of the Manchus. Yongling (originally known as Xingjingling) is located by the
Suzi River at the foot of the Qiyu Mountains in Hetuala city; Fuling is located on
Tianzhu Mountain on the north bank of the Hunhe River in the eastern suburbs of
Shenyang, so it is also called Eastern Tomb; Zhaoling is located five kilometers north
of Shenyang, so it is also called Northern Tomb.

永陵 原名兴京陵。陵区依山傍水，由前院、方城、宝城三部分组成，占地约1.2万平方米。陵内葬清太祖努尔哈赤的远祖盖特穆、曾祖福满、祖父觉世安，父塔克世等清皇室祖先。图中四座碑亭位于陵区前院，亭内各立一座颂扬墓主的神功圣德碑。

Yongling Originally called Xingjingling, the tomb covers 12,000 square meters and is composed of a front court, the "Square City" and the walled earth mound. The tomb preserves the remains of four ancestors of Nurhachi (Emperor Tai Zu of the Qing Dynasty). Each of the four pavilions in the front court shelters a stone tablet with an inscription recording the merits of the dead.

Mingqingjinshi
chenlieshi

Lishiwenwu
chenlieshi

启运殿
Qiyundian

明清金石陈列室　　历史文物陈列室

Xingzubeiting　　Qingzhaozu
beiting　　Jingzubeiting

兴祖碑亭　　清肇祖碑亭　　景祖碑亭
显祖碑亭
Xianzubeiting

Qiban
,zhubanfang

办公室
office　　齐班、祝版房

永 陵
YONGLING TOMBS

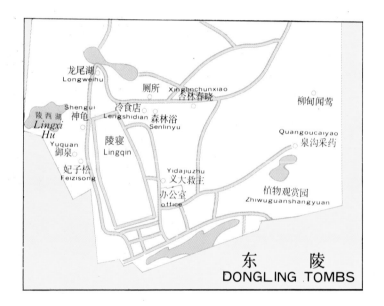

龙尾湖
Longweihu

厕所　　Xinglinchunxiao
杏林春晓

柳甸闻莺

冷食店
Lengshidian

陵西湖
Lingxi
Hu

Shengui
神龟

森林浴
Senlinyu

Quangoucaiyao
泉沟采药

Yuquan
御泉

陵寝
Lingqin

妃子松
Feizisong

Yidajiuzhu
义大救主

办公室
office

植物观赏园
Zhiwuguanshangyuan

东 陵
DONGLING TOMBS

福陵 清太祖努尔哈赤和皇后叶赫那拉氏的陵寝,因在沈阳市区之东,又名东陵。努尔哈赤(1559—1626年),女真族杰出首领,清王朝的奠基者。其陵前临浑河,后倚天柱山,万松耸翠,大殿凌云,构成独具风格的帝王山陵。图为福陵正红门。

Fuling It is the tomb of Nurhachi and his empress Yehenala. It is also known as Eastern Tomb because it is located to the east of Shenyang city. Nurhachi (1559-1626), was an outstanding chieftain of the Nüzhen tribe and the founder of the Qing Dynasty. The Hunhe River flows in front of his tomb and Tianzhu Mountain rises behind it. The picture shows the front gate of Fuling.

神道 即墓道。福陵神道在明清帝后陵中属特例，它依地势而起伏。图中一百零八阶砖磴，倚山势修筑而成，取意三十六天罡、七十二地煞。

Sacred Way The Sacred Way of Fuling runs up a mountain ridge while all other Sacred Ways in the imperial cemeteries of both the Ming and Qing dynasties are on flat ground. The Fuling Sacred Way's 108 brick-paved steps symbolize the 108 divine stars in heaven.

福陵碑楼　内立一石碑,碑文"大清福陵神功圣德碑"系康熙皇帝(1661－1722 年在位)亲撰,笔触矫健,气势磅礴,颇具帝王风范。

Stele Tower of Fuling　The stone tablet in the tower bears an inscription reading: "Divine Merit Stele of Fuling of the Great Qing". It was written by Emperor Kang Xi（1661-1722）. Kang Xi's handwriting is well known for its powerful and vigorous brushwork.

方城 为城堡式建筑，由长方形大青砖围合而成，城墙高约 7.6 米，周长 261 米，墙顶平坦，外侧修垛口，内侧砌矮墙。城南面正中为隆恩门，北面正中为明楼，四角有角楼，城内正中建有隆恩殿。方城是当时沈阳城的缩影。

"Square City" The castle-like structure is built with huge dark blue bricks. The wall around it is 7.6 meters high and 261 meters long. On the flat top of the wall there are parapets on the outer side and a breastwork on the inner side. A gate called Long'en is situated in the middle of the southern side and a tower rises on top of the wall in the middle of the northern side. Four towers stand on each corner of the "Square City". The Long'en Hall stands in the center of the "Square City". The "Square City" is a miniature of the Shenyang city of that time.

隆恩门 位于方城南面正中。城台上
三起门楼，楼上原有金链四条，寓示
江山万代。

Long'en Gate The tower-like gate is located in the middle of the southern side
of the "Square City". There used to be
four gold chains in the tower to imply
that the imperial rule would last forever.

隆恩殿 位于方城中央,建在雕刻精
美的花岗石台基上,宽三楹,辅以东
西配殿各五楹,雕梁画栋,富丽堂皇。
殿内为祭祀之所,供墓主神位。

Long'en Hall It stands in the middle of
the "Square City" on a granite terrace
with exquisite carvings in relief. On its
east and west are subsidiary halls with
painted beams and pillars. A memorial
tablet with the title of the dead emperor
is worshipped in the hall.

明楼 座落于方城北面城墙正中,为陵寝最高建筑。楼内立汉白玉石墓碑一通,上刻汉满蒙三种文字的"太祖高皇帝之陵"七个大字。明楼背后封土下即为墓室。

Memorial Tower (Minglou) The tower in the middle of the northern side of the "Square City" occupies the highest point of the burial ground. A white marble tablet in the tower is inscribed with the words: "Mausoleum of Emperor Tai Zu" in Chinese, Manchu and Mongolian languages. Behind the tower is an earth mound, under which is the burial chamber.

角楼 方城四隅各有一座角楼,是警卫官兵了望的地方。

Corner Tower On each corner of the "Square City" is a corner tower. It served as a guardhouse to protect the burial ground.

昭陵 清太宗皇太极（1626－1643 年在位）和皇后博尔济吉特氏的合葬陵，因位于沈阳城北，俗称北陵。制如福陵，是清初三陵中规模最大、体系最完整的一座。

Zhaoling The tomb for Huangtaiji (Emperor Tai Zong reigning from 1626 to 1643) and his empress Borqijite is located to the north of Shenyang proper, also known as Northern Tomb. The plan is the same as that of Fuling, but it is the largest of the Three Early Qing Tombs.

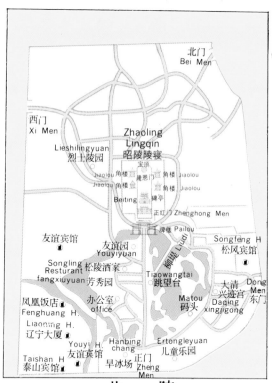

北　陵
BEILING TOMBS

隆恩殿内景　隆恩殿为陵寝正殿,内设大暖阁(又称寝宫)、小暖阁(又称佛龛)各一座。大暖阁前置帝、后龙凤宝座,座前设供桌,桌前置铜胎珐琅五供一套。进祭时,帝、后神牌分置龙凤宝座上,同案享供。

Inside Long'en Hall　It is the main hall of the imperial burial complex above the ground. Inside it there is a Greater Warm Chamber (also known as Bed Palace) and a Lesser Warm Chamber (also known as Buddha Shrine). Two thrones for the emperor and empress are placed before the Greater Warm Chamber. In front of the throne is a table on which a set of five altar-pieces is placed. At a sacrificial ceremony, the memorial tablets with the titles of the emperor and empress would be placed on the thrones.

东陵远眺 东陵位于河北省遵化县境内。北枕昌瑞山,东依倒仰山,西傍黄花山,前临西大河,黄瓦红墙掩映其中,自然景观与人文景观相映成趣,相得益彰。

Eastern Qing Tombs This group of Qing tombs is located in Zunhua County in Hebei Province. To its north are the Changrui Mountains, to its east are the Daoyang Mountains, and to its west are the Huanghua Mountains. The Xida River flows in front of it. The imperial tombs with their red walls and yellow glazed-tile roofs blend into the landscape in harmony.

孝陵 为东陵第一陵,居陵区中轴线,是清世祖爱新觉罗·福临(年号顺治,1643－1661 年在位)、孝康章皇后和孝献皇后的陵寝。顺治帝是清朝入关后第一位皇帝,其陵寝规模最大、体系最完整,在 5600 多米长的神道上,整齐有序地排列着石牌坊、大红门等十多组建筑。

Xiaoling The oldest of the Eastern Qing Tombs on the central axis is for Fulin (Emperor Shun Zhi who ruled from 1643 to 1661) and his empresses Xiaokang Zhang and Xiaoxian. Fulin was the first Qing emperor after the Manchus took Beijing. His tomb is the largest of Eastern Qing Tombs. On the 5,600-meter-long Sacred Way are a dozen buildings such as a stone archway and a magnificent gate.

石牌坊 孝陵第一座建筑,它标志着陵区的开始。牌坊通体由青白石雕刻而成,宽 31.35 米,高 12.48 米,五门六柱十一楼,是中国现存石牌坊中最宽的一座。

Stone Archway It is the first structure on the approach to Xiaoling. The archway of bluish white stone is 31.35 meters wide and 12.48 meters high. Six pillars divide the gate into five openings. It is the widest stone archway extant in China.

夹柱石浮雕 石牌坊雕刻以夹柱石上的双狮戏球图案最为精美,二狮一升一降,口衔绶带,锦地生风,活泼可爱。

Stone Relief Carvings The beautiful motif carved on the stone archway depicts two lovely lions playing with a ball. One lion is above the other, holding ribbons in their mouths.

大红门 孝陵门户,也是东陵总门户。门分三洞,为东陵现存建筑中唯一的一座庑殿顶建筑。两侧连接着环绕整个陵区的风水围墙。

Grand Palace Gate It is the front gate to Xiaoling and the main entrance to the whole ground of Eastern Qing Tombs. It is the only gate in this imperial cemetery without a gate tower. A high wall stretches from the gate to enclose the whole area.

大碑楼 即孝陵神功圣德碑亭。碑楼高峻挺拔,重檐歇山。内建石碑一通,由神兽赑屃托起,此兽性好负重,多用作碑跌。石碑上用满汉两种文字记载顺治帝一生的文治武功。

Grand Stele Tower This pavilion houses a stone tablet on a turtle-like mythical animal. An inscription in Chinese and Manchu languages on it records the merits of Emperor Shun Zhi. The pavilion has a high gabled roof with multiple eaves.

华表 大碑楼四角各竖汉白玉石华
表一座。中国的华表起源甚早,初为
木制,为纳谏而设,叫诽谤木。后来发
展成路标,称华表。现在的华表已无
原意,仅用以衬托主体建筑,使其更
加威严壮观。

Huabiao On each of the four corners of
the Grand Stele Tower stands an ornamented stone column called huabiao.
Huabiao used to be a wooden pole to
serve as a place where common people
could leave their complaints against local
officials. Then it became a road mark.
But in later times huabiao was used as an
ornamental object of stone.

望柱 中国古代称墓表。宋代(960—
1279年)以前均立于陵墓神道最前
面,为神道入口标志。明、清帝陵石牌
坊成为陵区第一道入口,望柱退居到
次要位置,变成一种纯装饰性标志。
图中孝陵望柱满刻云纹,纹饰端庄,
刀法隽秀,为石雕艺术中的上乘之
作。

Wangzhu The stone column was a
mark of entrance to a burial ground.
During the Song Dynasty (960-1279) it
was placed at the beginning of a Sacred
Way. During the Ming and Qing dynasties a stone archway replaced its original
function. Wangzhu thus became a purely
ornamental object. This wangzhu from
Xiaoling carved with cloud designs in relief is a masterpiece of stone sculpture
for its delicate workmanship.

大象 它温顺，又是力量的象征，置于神道，寓意皇帝广有顺民。孝陵大象，体形刚健，形象逼真，雕刻风格豪放，无造作之感。

Elephants The docile animal is a symbol of strength in China. It is placed on the Sacred Way to imply that the emperor abode by the wishes of the common people. The elephants at Xiaoling are powerful and life like.

武将 整体造型古朴敦厚，面部表情似笑非笑，于和蔼中隐含刚猛之气，显示出清初八旗大将的凛凛雄风。

Army Commanders The military officers have an expression with a subdued smile, hiding their toughness in mildness. The sculptures describe army commanders of the Manchu in the early days who had preserved many of their original nomadic characteristics.

石象生 东陵除惠陵外,各帝陵神道均排列石象生,孝陵最多,共十八对。由南向北井然有序地排列着狮子、狻猊、骆驼、大象、麒麟、马,卧立各一对;武将、文臣各三对。其雕刻技法古朴粗犷,表现出清初艺术的写意风格。

Stone Scupltures Except Huiling, each of the Eastern Qing Tombs has stone sculptures along its Sacred Way. Xiaoling has the largest number of them — 18 pairs altogether. They are arranged from south to north: lions, *suani* (a mythical animal), camels, elephants, Chinese unicorns, horses, army commanders and civil officials. The animals either stand or crouch. Six pairs are of human figures.

龙凤门 俗称"火焰牌楼"。门分三
道,中以琉璃影壁相接,六根门柱俱
由青白石雕制而成,形似华表而柱身
为正方形。石质额枋上雕有火焰宝
珠。整座建筑古朴而不失其华丽,庄
重而不失其轻巧。

Dragon-Phoenix Gate   The gate has
three openings. The central opening is
connected with a glazed-tile screen wall.
The six square pillars are made of bluish
white stone. On the horizontal board,
also of stone, are carvings of a ball surrounded by flames. The structure displays its extravagant and solemn beauty
through a simple design.

孝陵神道碑亭 为重檐歇山式建筑。内有石碑一通，上书顺治帝庙号和谥号。孝陵陵院建筑自此开始。

Stele Pavilion of Xiaoling The pavilion on the Sacred Way of Xiaoling has a gabled roof. A stone tablet in it bears the posthumous title of Emperor Shun Zhi. The pavilion is the beginning of the compound of Xiaoling.

隆恩门　位于神道正中,面阔五间,进深二间,单檐歇山式建筑。前开三洞大门,中门稍宽,叫神门,供帝后梓宫通行;左为君门,供皇帝祭奠时通行;右为臣门,王公大臣由此通行。隆恩门两侧连接着环绕整座陵院的红墙。

Long'en Gate　This gate in the middle of the Sacred Way has a gabled roof and three openings. The central opening is wider through which the coffin of the dead emperor was carried to the burial chamber. The opening on the left was used by the living emperor and the opening on the right was used by court officials. The wall to enclose the compound begins on either side of the gate.

西配殿壁画　西配殿位于隆恩门以北、隆恩殿西侧,是皇后忌辰喇嘛念经的地方。殿内有大型壁画一幅,形象地描绘了顺治九年(1652年)清世祖在北京西苑隆重接见达赖五世的情景。这次接见,缓和了清初激烈的民族矛盾,为确立清朝在西藏的统治奠定了基础。

Wall Paintings in Western Side Hall
The Western Side Hall to the north of Long'en Gate and to the west of Long'en Hall was where Buddhist monks held service for the dead empress. A painting on the wall inside it depicts the scene when Emperor Shun Zhi received the fifth Dalai Lama in 1652 in Beijing. This meeting alleviated the tension between the central government and Tibetan rulers.

鼎式炉 陈列于隆恩殿丹陛上,炉有双耳,三足为狻猊头;炉盖重檐,圆形攒尖,顶置宝珠。每遇祭奠,炉内燃香,烟雾缥缈。

Ding-Style Incense Burner The bronze burner on the marble terrace of Long'en Hall has two handles and three legs decorated with the head of suanni (a mythical animal). The lid of it tapers upward in several tiers with a ball on top. At sacrificial ceremonies incense was burned in it.

孝东陵 清朝第一座皇后陵,内葬孝惠章皇后及顺治帝的二十八名妃嫔。此陵开创了清朝皇后单独建陵之制,形成了清代皇后陵的基本格局。但体制不完善,将妃嫔也葬入陵内,构成皇后陵兼妃园寝的形式。陵园内孝惠章皇后宝顶前建方城明楼,明楼东西两侧纵向各排两行妃嫔宝顶,形成以皇后宝顶为中心,群星拱卫,唯我独尊的格局。

Eastern Xiaoling The tomb keeps the remains of Empress Xiaohui Zhang and 28 concubines of Emperor Shun Zhi. It set a precedent in the Qing Dynasty to build tombs exclusively for the emperor's wives. A tower stands on the "Square City" in front of the highest earth mound under which the two empresses are buried. Imperial concubines are buried under the earth mounds on either side of the large mound.

康熙皇帝画像

**Portrait of Emperor
Kang Xi.**

景陵 清朝第三位皇帝康熙帝陵寝。
康熙帝在位六十一年,他久战沙场,
励精图治,出现了"康乾盛世"的繁荣
景象。其陵首创双碑、牌楼门等建筑
形式,规模宏大,布局严整集中,工艺
更趋完美。图为从景陵宝城看明楼。

Jingling This tomb is for Kang Xi,
third emperor of the Qing Dynasty. He
was a brave soldier and wise leader.
China became prosperous under his 61
years' reign. His tomb was the first to
have two stone memorial tablets and a
front gate like a palace hall. The complex is large in scale and beautifully designed. The picture shows the tomb surrounded by a high wall.

裕陵双碑 圣德神功碑建双碑始于康熙景陵。乾隆皇帝在位年久,文治武功,显赫一世,号称"十全老人"。为彰其德,亦立双碑,左满文,右汉文。碑文由嘉庆帝御撰,字体由乾隆第十一子、清代著名书法家成亲王永瑆书写,洋洋洒洒,4300余字,极尽歌功颂德之能事。

Twin Steles of Yuling China was in peace and prosperity under the 60 years' reign of Emperor Qian Long. Emperor Jia Qing wrote a eulogy to him. Prince Yong Xing, a famous calligrapher and 11th son of Emperor Qian Long, inscribed the eulogy of 4,300 characters on the stone tablets in Manchu and Chinese languages.

裕陵 清朝第六位皇帝乾隆帝的陵寝。乾隆帝二十五岁登基,在位六十年,又当了三年太上皇,八十九岁去世,是中国封建帝王中掌权最久、享寿最高的皇帝。乾隆年间国库充盈,兴建裕陵历时五十余年,其规模、质量在清帝陵中均属上乘。

Yuling It is the tomb of Qian Long, sixth emperor of the Qing Dynasty. Qian Long ascended to the throne at 25, stayed there for 60 years, then retired to become the Super-Sovereign for three years before he died at 89. He ruled and lived the longest of time among Chinese emperors. The construction of his tomb continued for over 50 years. It is one of the best and the largest of Qing Tombs.

乾隆皇帝画像

Portrait of Emperor
Qian Long.

地宫 图为裕陵地宫，它是清陵所有已开放地宫中最壮观、最豪华、最复杂的。由九券四门组成，券顶、券壁和石门上雕有菩萨、天王等佛教石刻，堪称地下佛堂。

Underground Palace The picture shows the burial chamber of Yuling. It is the most complex and lavishly decorated burial chamber of the Qing Tombs so far excavated. On the arched ceilings of the four entrances to it there are relief carvings describing Buddhist images.

文殊菩萨雕像 雕在地宫第一道石门西侧。像高1.5米，头顶莲花佛冠，身披缨络菊花宝珠，赤脚立于出水芙蓉之上。雕刻细腻生动，具有较高艺术价值。

Relief Carving of Manjusri Carved on the western wall of the tunnel of the first entrance the portrait of the Bodhisattva is 1.5 meters high wearing a lotus flower crown and a robe laced with pearls. It stands on a water lily blossom barefooted. The carving of excellent craftsmanship is of high artistic value.

持国天王雕像 刻在地宫首门洞券内。他以琵琶为法器，守护着佛经中须弥山的东方。

Relief Carving of Dhrtarastra Carved on the wall of the first entrance to the burial chamber, the Buddhist god holds a *pipa* lute as a weapon. He is the guardian of the eastern part of the world.

狮子进宝 狮子在中国被视为百兽之王。裕陵地宫雕刻的这头雄狮,背驮宝瓶进贡,寓意皇家威震天下,统摄四方。

Lion Presents Treasure In China the lion is regarded as the king of animals. This stone lion in the burial chamber of Yuling carries a precious bottle to present to the dead emperor, meaning that the royal power was the highest.

地宫金券 为地宫最后一券,是安放帝后梓宫之处。内设宝床,上置乾隆皇帝及五位后妃的棺椁。1928 年孙殿英盗陵,两棺被毁,现仅存四具,尸骨均在棺内。

Burial Chamber The last vault of the burial chamber of Yuling keeps the cof-fins of Emperor Qian Long and his five consorts. In 1928 warlord Sun Dianying plundered Yuling and destroyed two coffins. The four remaining coffins still have the remains of the royal members.

焚帛炉 祭祀时烧化祝版、制帛等祭祀品的地方。妃园寝规制低于帝后陵,其焚帛炉之琉璃构件用较低等级的绿色,且只在东侧设一座。

Sacrificial Silk Burners Two sacrificial Silk burners are found in front of every tomb for an emperor. Only one is placed on the eastern side of an imperial concubine tomb. It is made of glazed pottery in green color.

妃园寝 清代妃嫔的墓葬群，此制始于康熙朝。图为裕陵妃园寝，内葬乾隆皇帝三十六位后妃。裕妃陵设东西配殿，建方城明楼，超越了规制。

Tombs of Imperial Concubines During the reign of Emperor Kang Xi, special grounds were set aside for imperial concubines in the imperial cemeteries. The picture shows the imperial concubine tomb at Yuling, which keeps the remains of 36 concubines of Emperor Qian Long. The tomb has two wing halls and a front tower, an addition to the tomb exceeding the status of imperial concubines.

宝顶群 裕妃园寝后院，顺序排列三十五个宝顶，其下埋葬着乾隆皇帝的三十六位后妃。宝顶位置先后、规模大小皆显示出墓主生前地位的尊卑。

Earth Mounds Under the 35 earth mounds in the backyard of the imperial concubine tomb are the remains of 36 imperial concubines of Emperor Qian Long. The mounds vary in height and size according to the status of the dead under them.

纯惠皇贵妃地宫 为皇贵妃地宫之
典型,计有五券一门。金券内石床正
中为纯惠皇贵妃棺枢,其右停放那拉
皇后棺椁。那拉皇后于乾隆三十年
(1765 年)随帝南巡时惹恼了皇帝,从
此失宠,死后仅以皇贵妃礼葬入妃园
寝,未建单独的宝顶地宫,且棺椁摆
在卑位,尚不如一般妃嫔。

Burial Chamber of Lady Chunhui   The
burial chamber is composed of five
arched vaults and one gate. The coffin
of Lady Chunhui is placed on a stone
platform in the last vault. On its right is
the coffin of Empress Nala. Empress
Nala lost favor of Emperor Qian Long
and was buried with an imperial concubine when she died. There is no separate
earth mound for her above the ground.

香妃地宫 为清代典型的妃型地宫。香妃是一位极富传奇色彩的女子。相传她不假熏沐而体有异香。史实中的香妃即乾隆的容妃,是一位为民族团结做出过贡献的维吾尔族女子,五十五岁卒,葬入妃园寝。

Burial Chamber of Lady Xiangfei Xiangfei, according to legend, emitted a nice scent from her body without applying perfume. She was a Uygur girl who became an imperial concubine of Emperor Qian Long and died at the age of 55. She is remembered for her endeavor to close the relations between central government and the Uygur people.

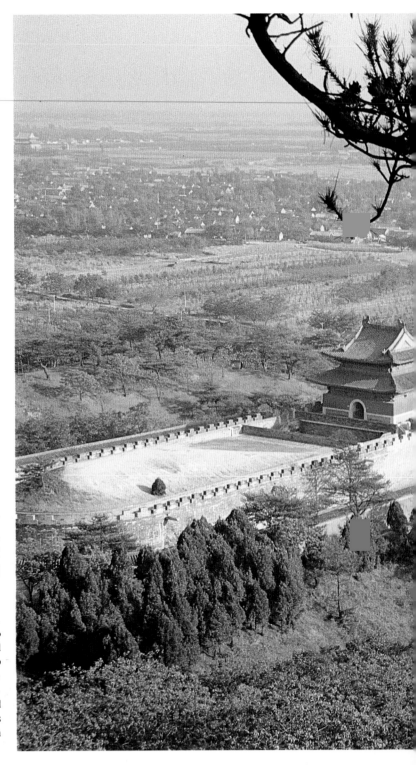

定陵远眺 清朝第九位皇帝咸丰帝
（1850—1861 年在位）的陵寝。定陵地
势峻峭，落差较大，自石象生至罗圈
墙仅 300 余米，建筑物设置紧凑，图
为从后山前眺定陵全景。

Dingling The tomb of Xian Feng,
ninth emperor of the Qing Dynasty who
was on the throne between 1850 and
1861, is situated on a steep
mountainside. The buildings are arranged in a compact layout. The dis-
tance between the stone sculptures and
the wall surrounding the earth mound is
only 300 meters. This picture was taken
from the mountain behind the tomb.

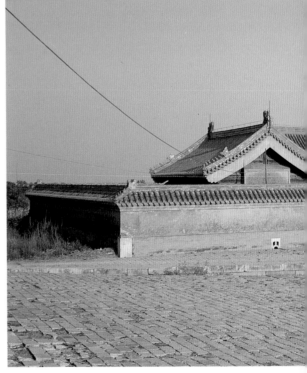

牌楼门 位于石象生以北,五间六柱十一楼,属点缀建筑,系景陵首创。图为定陵牌楼门。

Archway Tower The archway tower to the north of the stone sculptures at Dingling has five openings separated by six pillars. The first archway in the form of a tower was built at Jingling.

神厨库　位于神道碑亭以东,红墙环绕,自成一院,院内迎门有神厨五间,是制作肉食祭品的地方。南北各三间为神库,是存放神厨祭品及原料之处。

Offerings Kitchen　It is located to the east of the Stele Pavilion on the Sacred Way and surrounded by a red wall. The kitchen was used to cook the meat for a sacrificial ceremony. To its south and north there are storehouses for keeping tools and raw materials.

隆恩殿 咸丰皇帝在位时饱经战乱，国库空虚，致使营建陵寝经费不足，不得已而使用修建道光陵时废弃的旧料，虽如此，定陵大殿仍不失皇陵巍峨之貌。

Long'en Hall The main memorial hall of Dingling, tomb of Emperor Xian Feng, was built with leftover materials for the construction of the tomb of Emperor Dao Guang because a shortage of funds. China was in trouble of constant war during his reign. Still the hall shows the grandness of an imperial building.

隆恩殿内景　清陵以清明、孟秋望、冬至、岁暮、帝后忌辰为五大祭，多由王公致祭，有时皇帝也亲临主持。图中表现的是同治十二年（1873年）皇帝主持大祭礼的情景。持香行礼者为同治皇帝。

Inside Long'en Hall　Five grand sacrificial ceremonies were held at the imperial cemetery in a year. Most of them were presided by princes. The living emperor appeared only occasionally. The picture depicts Emperor Tong Zhi at a sacrificial ceremony held in 1873.

省牲亭 位于神厨库院内东南角，为宰杀祭祀用牛羊之处。内设锅灶及厨房用具等。

Slaughterhouse It is located in the southeastern corner in the compound of the Offerings Kitchen. Cattle and sheep were killed here for sacrifice.

东配殿 位于焚帛炉北，是存放祭祀祝版、祝帛的殿堂。逢隆恩殿大修，亦临时存放墓主牌位。图为定陵东配殿。

Eastern Side Hall The hall to the north of the sacrificial paper burner served as a storehouse for sacrificial papers. When the main memorial hall was under repair, memorial tablets with the dead emperor's titles were moved here. The picture shows the Eastern Side Hall of Dingling.

明楼 定陵地势陡峭，从五供仰视明楼，愈显气势雄浑。

Memorial Tower of Dingling It rises high above the front gate of the wall surrounding the earth mound at Dingling.

明楼翼角彩画　额枋为烟琢墨石碾玉旋子彩画，斗栱为金琢墨彩画，轮廓线镀金，红帮绿底，美而不俗。

Painted Eaves of Memorial Tower　The rafters of the tower are painted with spirals and the brackets with red and green motifs bordered by gold lines.

五供基座雕刻　五供基座为须弥座，上坊雕缠枝西番莲，下坊雕暗八仙、八宝，寓意众神众佛将最珍贵最灵验的礼物奉献给皇帝。整个基座雕工精细，图纹生动，具有很强的表现力。

Altar-Piece Dais　Five altar-pieces are placed on a stone dais carved with flower designs on the upper part and on the lower part the Eight Immortals, each holding a precious present for the dead emperor. The relief sculpture is of high craftsmanship.

月牙城　为方城券洞北的月牙形院落,其北墙正中琉璃影壁处是地宫入口。为防止泄密,雇用哑巴在此施工,俗称哑巴院。

Crescent Castle　It is a courtyard in the shape of a crescent inside the wall and in front of the earth mound. A screen wall of glazed tiles is the beginning of a tunnel to the underground burial chamber. The builders of the tomb were mutes who could not tell the secrets of the tomb. So the courtyard is also called "Mutes' Yard".

七星沟漏 设于月牙城地面的渗水孔。匠人在大理石上凿七个古钱状的排水沟漏,将积水汇于地下月牙沟排出,保持陵院干燥。自道光陵以后各陵均设有与此相同的排水系统。

Seven-Star Water Gargoyles Rain water is drained through seven holes in marble blocks at the ground level in the courtyard of the tomb. Such drainage system was invented during the reign of Emperor Dao Guang.

月牙河 位于大殿和明楼磋礓之间,直接与地宫暗沟相连,后寝和地宫积水由此排出。其状如月牙,故称月牙河。

Crescent River The ditch between Long'en Hall and Memorial Tower is connected to the underground drainage system. Water is drained through this ditch from the tomb.

挡水坝 即陵寝后边两段弧形石墙。每至雨季，山洪夹杂沙石自上而下，冲击山陵，挡水坝将其截住，使之向两侧分流。

Water Dam Two semicircular walls stand on each side of the tomb to block off and divert any runoff of rain water from the mountainside behind the tomb.

宝顶 定陵在清帝陵修造上承前启后，其宝顶改变了传统做法，把金券垒成庑殿蓑衣顶，然后用三合土夯成长圆形宝顶。

"Precious Top" Tombs of earlier Qing emperors had an arched ceiling. Dingling began to have a gabled and hipped roof over the burial chamber. After the underground chamber was finished, a mixture of earth and lime was piled on the roof to form a mound, which was called "Precious Top".

定东陵 是咸丰皇帝两位皇后慈安和慈禧的陵寝。两陵间仅隔一条马槽沟,建筑规制和修建年代相同。光绪二十一年(1895年),慈禧太后以年久失修为由,令重修其陵,历时十四年完工,使慈安陵相形见绌。

Eastern Dingling This mausoleum is composed of two tombs, built in 1895, one for Ci An and one for Ci Xi, two empresses of Emperor Xian Feng. They were of the same plan, separated by a ditch. Ci Xi ordered to rebuild her tomb at the pretext that it was in disrepair. The project was finished in 14 years. Ci Xi's tomb became much more impressive than that of Ci An.

慈禧太后 慈禧太后于清末独揽朝纲达四十八年之久，是中国近代史上的传奇人物，图为她着朝服的像。

Empress Dowager Ci Xi Empress Dowager Ci Xi made the emperor a puppet while she held the actual power for 48 years. This is a portrait of her in ceremonial dress.

慈禧陵 图中隆恩殿的梁枋架木、门窗隔扇均采用名贵花梨木建造，古色古香。殿前丹陛石，凤在上龙在下，采用高浮雕加透雕手法，构思新颖，技法高超。

Ci Xi's Tomb The beams, rafters and windows of Long'en Hall are made of precious pear wood. The relief carving on a stone block in front of the hall has a dragon and a phoenix. Against the long tradition which puts the dragon above the phoenix, the design at Ci Xi's tomb has the phoenix riding above the dragon.

蚣蝮 传为龙子之一,性喜水,常被用于古建筑物的排水沟口,慈禧陵隆恩殿丹陛周围共设六只,既可排水,又有装饰作用。

Paxia According to Chinese mythology, paxia is one of the nine sons of the dragon. It loves water. So its image is often seen at a water outlet. There are six gargoyles on the stone foundation of Long'en Hall in the shape of a paxia.

石雕 隆恩殿周围汉白玉石栏杆上,浮雕六十九幅龙凤呈祥、水浪流云图案。彩凤在前展翅飞翔,蛟龙在后振爪奋追,其情其景是同治、光绪两朝慈禧太后专权的艺术再现。

Stone Carvings Relief carvings on the marble balusters around Long'en Hall depict 69 pairs of dragon and phoenix playing amidst water waves and clouds. The phoenix surges ahead of the dragon, symbolizing that Empress Dowager Ci Xi was leading the country during the reign of Emperor Tong Zhi and Emperor Guang Xi.

和玺彩画 清陵建筑多饰旋子彩画，唯慈禧陵三殿梁枋绘有和玺彩画，彩画用金箔镶贴出二龙戏珠、寿字等不同图案，线条繁密细腻，风格典雅华美，表现了清代彩画的高超技艺。图为隆恩殿内彩画。

Decorative Motifs   Most of buildings in the Qing Tombs bear decorative motifs of spirals on pillars, beams and windows. But the motifs on Sanliang Hall at Ci Xi's tomb are two dragons playing a ball or in the shape of a Chinese character for longevity. The picture shows the painted motifs inside Long'en Hall.

砖雕 隆恩殿内壁磨砖雕花，有"五蝠捧寿"、"四角盘肠"、"卍字不到头"等吉祥图案。砖雕外围，饰以蔓草莲花和珠纹，并以黄金装饰，奢侈豪华，富丽堂皇。

Brick Carvings   The well-polished bricks lining the inside of the wall of Long'en Hall are carved in relief with auspicious patterns such as "Five Bats at Birthday Celebration", "Twisting Ribbons Around the Four Corners" and continuous links of the symbol for longevity. Around the carving is gilded motifs of lotus flowers and pearls.

隆恩殿内景 光绪三十年（1904年），慈禧太后七十大寿，曾扮成观音大士，端坐于莲花台上。头戴昆罗帽，外套五佛冠，身披团花寿纹袍，右手持佛珠。左侧李莲英扮善财童子，右侧奕劻之女四格格扮龙女。前为荷花丛，后为紫竹林。蜡像所塑人物栩栩如生。

Inside Long'en Hall At her 70th birthday celebration in 1904, Empress Dowager Ci Xi dressed up as Guanyin (Goddess of Mercy) in a Buddhist crown and robe and holding a string of beads. The wax figures in Long'en Hall describe the scene on the occasion. Ci Xi sits on a lotus flower seat. Her favorite eunuch Li Lianying stands on her left and the fourth daughter of Prince Yikuang stands on her right. In front of her is a cluster of lotus flowers and behind her is a group of bamboo.

慈禧太后地宫 典型的后陵地宫,五券二门,雕刻华美,选料精良。陵院有完整的排水系统,建筑设计更趋合理。

Burial Chamber for Ci Xi The chamber is built with fine materials and composed of five vaults and two gates with fine relief carvings. The tomb is kept dry with a perfect drainage system.

慈禧太后棺椁 分为两层,外层为椁,金丝楠木制作,涂漆四十九道,最外层是金漆,漆上是喇嘛用藏文书写的经咒,旨在超度亡灵。里层为棺,红漆填金。1928年孙殿英盗陵,慈禧太后尸骨被抛出棺外,后经考古人员整理放于棺内。

Conffins of Ci Xi The remains of Empress Dowager Ci Xi are placed in two coffins one inside the other. Made of precious nanmu wood, the coffins were painted with 49 layers of lacquer. The outmost coating was mixed with gold powder and inscribed with Buddhist scriptures in Tibetan language. In 1928 warlord Sun Dianying blew open the tomb to loot the treasures inside. The remains of Ci Xi were scattered. Later archaeologists collected the remains and put them back in the confin.

祭器 均为瓷器,皇家祭陵专用品。系景德镇官窑产品,质地细腻,釉子肥润。

Sacrificial Objects All made of porcelain, they were used at sacrificial ceremonies at the Qing Tombs. The fine porcelain articles were produced at an official kiln in Jingdezhen, Jiangxi Province.

纱袍 为慈禧太后夏装,制作者在淡褐纱地上平织竹叶,中间夹杂用金线织成的团寿字。她十分喜欢此袍,六十九岁大寿穿着照相留念,现存于慈禧太后陵神厨库内。

Gauze Robe The summer wear of Empress Dowager Ci Xi is inlaid with patterns of bamboo leaves and the Chinese character for longevity of gold filaments. Ci Xi posed for a picture in it on her 59th birthday. The robe is kept in Offerings Kitchen on the Sacred Way to her tomb.

饰物 宫廷用品,有香珠、香袋、荷包等,多为满清贵族佩带。质地为紫金锭,香味扑鼻。

Ornaments Among the magnitude of ornamental articles in the imperial palace of the Qing Dynasty are strings of pearls, perfume bags and embroidered pouches. They give off a nice scent.

惠陵 清朝第十位皇帝同治帝(1861－1874年在位)之陵。始建于光绪元年(1875年),历时三年完工,是清朝各帝陵中施工期最短的陵寝。惠陵裁撤了通往孝陵的神路和石象生、圣德神功碑楼、二柱门等建筑,在东陵诸帝陵中最朴。

Huiling It is the tomb of Tong Zhi, 10th emperor of the Qing Dynasty who was on the throne from 1861 to 1874. Construction began in 1875 and was finished in three years, the shortest construction time of the Qing Tombs. It does not have the usual Sacred Way to connect it with the main tomb of Xiaoling, the Divine Merit Stele Tower or the Twin-Pillar Gate. It is the simplest of the Eastern Qing Tombs.

昭西陵 是清太宗皇太极的孝庄文
皇后之陵。她曾先后辅佐两代幼主开
基创业。卒于康熙二十六年（1687
年），因其辈份高于孝陵陵主顺治帝，
故葬于陵区大红门外。从地理位置
看，此陵位于沈阳皇太极的昭陵之
西，故名昭西陵。在清代诸陵中，帝、
后陵相距千里，实属特例。

Western Zhaoling It is the tomb of
Empress Xiaozhuang Wen of Emperor
Tai Zu (Huangtaiji). The capable empress helped two young emperors (one
her son, the other her grandson) consol-
idate their power. Her tomb is located to
the west of Zhaoling in Shenyang city,
so it is called Western Zhaoling.

孝庄文皇后朝服像

Portrait of Empress Xiaozhuang Wen in
her ceremonial clothes.

清　西　陵

　　清西陵占地 800 多平方公里,陵区内建有四座帝陵,三座后陵,三座妃陵以及四座公主、皇子和王爷陵,其中分别埋葬着四位皇帝,九位皇后,五十七位妃嫔,六位公主、皇子和王爷,总计七十六人。

　　清西陵兴建于中国最末一个封建王朝的后期,建筑技艺已臻成熟和完美。各陵均依据墓主生前意愿而建,所以形式多样,风格各异。这里是中国陵寝模式最集中、最具代表性的陵区。泰陵以其规模宏大、体系完整居清代众帝陵之首。慕陵无方城明楼,看似简朴,实则耗资最巨,用工甚众,其建筑式样在诸陵中最有特色。唯昌陵别具一格,整个隆恩殿用珍贵的花斑石镶贴,如宝石铺地,满堂生辉,堪称中国古建一绝。崇陵虽匆匆而建,但大殿梁柱均选用上等铁木为料,素有"铜梁铁柱"之称,颇具皇陵雄姿。

　　清西陵陵区群峰并立,古木葱茏,各陵背山面水,松柏拱卫,风景甚是美丽,是北京西行第一处旅游胜地。

The Western Qing Tombs

　　The entire complex occupies an area of 800 square kilometers including four tombs for emperors, three tombs for empresses, three tombs for imperial concubines and four tombs for princes and princesses. Four emperors, nine empresses, 57 imperial concubines and six princes and princesses are buried here.

　　The Western Qing Tombs were built in the latter part of the Qing Dynasty. Architectural techniques had become very advanced. Each living emperor designed his own tomb in the style he liked. So the Western Qing Tombs look different from one another. Tailing, the chief tomb of the cemetery, is the largest and mostly elaborated; Muling, without a "Square City" and Memorial Tower, looks simple from outside but it cost the largest amount of money; Long'en Hall of Changling is lined all over with expensive granophyer slabs as if the floor were paved with precious stones; the beams and pillars of the main hall of Congling are of high-quality ironwood.

　　The whole area of the Western Qing Tombs are surrounded by high mountain peaks. Each tomb is sheltered by mountains with a river flowing in front of it. In its vicinity there are ancient pine and cypress trees. Today the Western Qing Tombs are the number one tourist attraction to the west of Beijing.

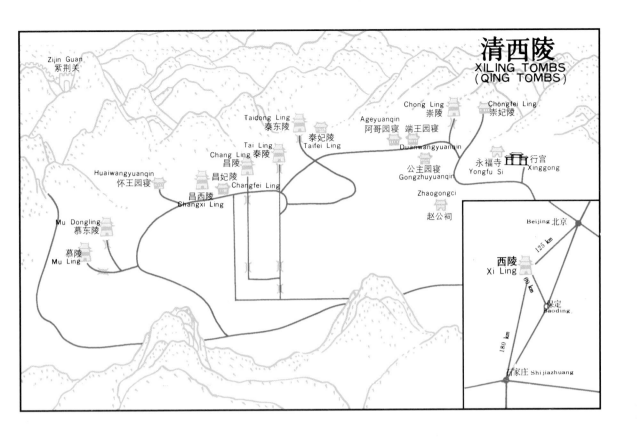

清西陵
XILING TOMBS
(QING TOMBS)

Zijin Guan 紫荆关

Taidong Ling 泰东陵
泰妃陵 Taifei Ling

Chong Ling 崇陵
Chongfei Ling 崇妃陵

Tai Ling 泰陵
Chang Ling 昌陵
Ageyuanqin 阿哥园寝 端王园寝 Duanwangyuanqin

Huaiwangyuanqin 怀王园寝
昌妃陵 Changfei Ling
昌西陵 Changxi Ling

公主园寝 Gongzhuyuanqin

永福寺 Yongfu Si 行宫 Xinggong

Zhaogongci 赵公祠

Mu Dongling 慕东陵

慕陵 Mu Ling

Beijing 北京
西陵 Xi Ling
125 km
90 km
保定 Baoding
180 km
石家庄 Shijiazhuang

泰陵 清西陵第一陵,内葬清朝第五位皇帝雍正帝(1722－1735 年在位)和孝敬宪皇后及敦肃皇贵妃。雍正皇帝是清代"康乾盛世"承前启后的关键人物,为清代中期的昌盛做出了较大贡献,称得上贤明之君,故泰陵在清西陵中规模最大。

Tailing The oldest and largest of the Western Qing Tombs keeps the remains of Yong Zheng (fifth emperor of the Qing Dynasty who ruled between 1722 and 1735) and his empresses Xiaojing Xian and Dunsu. Under the capable administration of Yong Zheng China became prosperous. He is remembered in China as a wise ruler.

五孔桥 西陵共有石桥四十九座，其中泰陵五孔桥最为壮观。它长 87 米，宽 10.94 米，拱高 4.9 米，由长方形青白石砌成，如长虹垂地，气势雄伟。

Five-Arch Bridge There are altogether 49 bridges in the area of the Western Qing Tombs. The Five-Arch Bridge at Tailing is the most magnificent. Built of bluish stone slabs, it is 87 meters long, 10.94 meters wide and 4.9 meters high.

128

泰陵碑楼 雍正皇帝在位时,勤于朝政,国事盛昌。乾隆二年(1737年)修建这座碑楼,以颂扬其功德。楼内赑屃驮碑,额曰"大清泰陵圣德神功碑"。碑楼四角各立华表一座,将大碑楼衬托得更加巍峨雄伟。

Stele Tower of Tailing The Stele Tower was erected in 1737 as a tribute to Emperor Yong Zheng for his diligent and fruitful administration. The upper part of the stone stele is inscribed with "Divine Merit Stele of Tailing of the Great Qing". Four ornamented stone columns at the four corners enhance the magnificence of the tower.

石牌坊　西陵有七座牌坊,其中石质五座,木石结构二座。图为泰陵牌坊院,院由三座雕刻精美的石牌坊组成,一座居中横跨神道,二座稍后分列左右。它们矗立在宽敞的平野上,历二百余年风雨沧桑,雄姿不减当年。

Stone Archway　Of the seven archways in the Western Qing Tombs five are of stone and two of wood. The picture shows the Archway Compound at Tailing. Three stone archways in it rise high on a flat open lot with the central one spanning the Sacred Way. They have preserved their original grandeur after 200 years.

龙凤门　位于石象生北,三门六柱三楼四壁。其顶脊、斗拱、梁枋等均由彩色琉璃件组成,雍容华贵,给人以穿门入户之感,愈显神道深远、陵区肃穆。

Dragon-Phoenix Gate　The gate to the north of the stone sculptures looks like a palace hall. Its roof ridges, beams and brackets are made of glazed tiles. Six pillars divide the gate into three openings.

琉璃彩龙 龙凤门正面四壁中心各嵌盘龙一条，背面各饰琉璃鸳鸯荷花一组，象征帝后同穴，生死合好。

Glazed-Pottery Dragon Inlaid in each of the four walls of the front side of Dragon-Phoenix Gate is a coiling dragon on a background of mandarin ducks and lotus flowers, also made of glazed pottery. The pattern symbolizes the union of the emperor and his empress.

石象生 泰陵石象生共五对,依次为狮子、大象、骏马、文臣、武将。它们两两相对分列于神道两旁,颇似仪仗守卫在陵前。

Stone Sculptures There are five pairs of stone sculptures along each side of the Sacred Way: lions, elephants, horses, civil court officials and military court officials. They serve as honorary guards of the dead emperor.

象背浮雕 大象饰鞍鞯、驮宝瓶,与清代前期孝陵石象自然古朴的雕刻技法截然不同,显得奢华和造作。象驮宝瓶,称为"太平有象",寓意国泰民安。

Relief Carvings on Elephants The stone elephants at the Western Qing Tombs are much more elaborately carved than those found in earlier Qing imperial cemeteries. The elephant carries a precious bottle on its saddled back, a symbol of peace.

隆恩殿内景 泰陵隆恩殿为重檐歇山顶,面阔五间,进深三间,其外形与其他隆恩殿大同小异,但殿内四根明柱别有特色,柱身金龙、盘花缠绕,沥粉贴金,华贵异常。殿正中设金漆御凤宝座,至今保存完好。

Inside Long'en Hall Long'en Hall of Tailing has a gabled roof with multiple eaves. Its design is similar to that of other imperial tombs. But the four pillars inside this hall are different: they have gilded dragons and flower motifs on them. The throne is placed in the center of the hall.

琉璃花门　即陵寝门,系后寝大门,
为门楼式建筑。楼脊和墙面均由琉璃
构件镶砌而成,色彩绚丽,雍容华贵。

Glazed-Tile Gate　The tower-like gate is
the entrance to the burial chamber. Its
roof and wall are lined with colorful
glazed tiles.

二柱门　建于琉璃门北，为木石结构。既为明楼前装饰，又似华表以示墓主身价不凡。

Twin-Pillar Gate　The gate to the north of the Glazed-Tile Gate is built of stone and wood. It is an ornamental object in front of the Memorial Tower and a symbol of the status of the dead.

泰陵古松　清西陵松柏始栽于建陵之初，整个陵区共有古松柏二十余万株。遥望乔松巨柏，参天蔽日，颇有"翠海"之感。

Ancient Pines at Tailing　There are altogether 200,000 pine and cypress trees at the Western Qing Tombs. They were planted during the construction of an imperial tomb. The picture shows ancient pine trees at Tailing.

泰东陵 位于泰陵东北 1.5 公里处，雍正皇帝的孝圣宪皇后陵寝。清制，皇后先于皇帝驾薨者与皇帝合葬，后于皇帝驾薨者另建陵寝。孝圣宪皇后去世时，泰陵地宫已闭封三十九年，故另葬他处。陵寝主要建筑有隆恩门、东西配殿、隆恩殿、方城明楼、宝顶地宫等，在清代后陵中规模较大。

Eastern Tailing Located 1.5 kilometers to the northeast of Tailing, this tomb was built for Empress Xiaosheng Xian of Emperor Yong Zheng. According to Qing customs when the empress died before the emperor her body would be kept and buried with the emperor when the latter died. If the empress died after the emperor her body would be buried separately. When Empress Xiaosheng Xian died her emperor had died 39 years earlier. Her tomb is the largest of those for empresses of the Qing Dynasty, complete with Long'en Gate, side halls, Long'en Hall, walled mound and lavishly decorated burial chamber.

泰陵妃园寝 位于泰东陵东南 1 公里处，为雍正帝二十一个妃嫔的墓葬群。地面建筑主要有隆恩门、东西配殿、隆恩殿、琉璃门等，没有方城明楼，但增建了配殿，是一点小小的逾制。

Concubine Tombs at Tailing Twenty-one concubines of Emperor Yong Zheng are buried in a compound one kilometer southeast of Eastern Tailing. Structures above the ground include Long'en Gate, side halls, Long'en Hall and Glazed-Tile Gate. But there are no memorial halls.

泰东陵宝顶 宝顶下葬乾隆帝生母孝圣宪皇后。史载,乾隆皇帝对她"晨昏问侍,扶掖安辇,极尊养之,隆祝礼让,善至于终身。"年八十六而薨,是清朝享寿最高的皇太后。

Earth Mound of Eastern Tailing Empress Xiaosheng Xian, mother of Emperor Qian Long, is buried under the earth mound. Emperor Qian Long would pay his respect to his mother in the morning and at evening every day. When she went out the emperor would walk along her carriage. The empress dowager died at 86, the longest life led by Qing empresses.

昌陵　清朝第七位皇帝嘉庆帝（1796
－1820年在位）的陵寝。此陵整体建
筑与泰陵大体一致，但其大碑楼、隆
恩门、明楼、宝城等建筑比泰陵还高
大壮观。

Changling　It is the tomb of Jia Qing,
seventh emperor of the Qing Dynasty
who ruled from 1796 to 1820. It is the
same in size as Tailing but its Stele Tower, Long'en Hall, Memorial Hall and
the earth mound are higher than those of
Tailing.

昌陵隆恩殿 从明楼看隆恩殿,大殿重檐垂脊,黄瓦朱墙,挺拔宏阔,蔚为壮观。

Long'en Hall of Changling The grand hall has a roof with steep ridges and multiple eaves. The roof is covered with yellow glazed tiles. The wall is painted in red.

隆恩殿地面 为稀有紫花石铺就,此种石料产于河南省,经磨制后每块呈正方形,抛光烫蜡,不滑不涩。石面紫色花纹似春蚕、若芙蓉、象竹笋、如绒球,千姿百态,美不胜收。若被阳光照射,五彩生辉,犹如满堂宝石。此种地面,在诸多皇陵中独一无二。

Floor of Long'en Hall The floor is paved with a rare kind of stone called "Purple Flower Stone". The stone from Henan Province was carefully polished and waxed. Walking on it one does not feel slippery or hard-going. The veins in the stone resemble silkworms, lotus blossoms, bamboo stalks or fluffy balls. They reflect dazzling colors in sunlight. Of all the Qing Tombs Changling is the only one whose Long'en Hall is thus paved.

昌陵明楼 其外形与其他清陵明楼无异，但高出 50 多厘米，为诸陵之首。

Memorial Tower of Changling This tower is the same in structure as those of other imperial tombs but is 50 centimeters taller.

明楼石碑 碑基为汉白玉石须弥座，座上有游龙浮雕；碑身以朱砂涂面，碑额为二龙戏珠浮雕。石碑正面用满汉蒙三种文字浮雕"仁宗睿皇帝之陵"七个大字。

Stone Tablet in the Memorial Tower The base of the marble tablet is carved with swimming dragons in relief. The tablet itself is painted in red and inscribed with "Mausoleum of Emperor Ren Zong" in the front side in Manchu, Mongolian and Chinese languages. On top of the tablet is a relief carving of two dragons playing with a pearl.

昌陵宝城 图中城墙绕墓一周，墙内隆起的巨大土丘下便是停放嘉庆皇帝棺椁的地宫。昌陵地宫至今未开。据"雷氏图纸"考证，地宫为四门九券，遍刻佛像经文，是一座稀有的石雕艺术宝库和庄严肃穆的地下佛堂。

Earth Mound of Changling The mound is surrounded by a high wall. The burial chamber under the mound has not been excavated. But according to history records, the burial chamber has four gates. The walls of the gateways are inscribed with Buddhist scriptures. Archaeologists predict that the tomb will turn out to be a treasurehouse of stone sculpture.

龙亭 停放在昌西陵隆恩殿内,为装载亡灵牌位的亭子。

Dragon Pavilion The small pavilion inside Long'en Hall of Changling keeps the wooden memorial tablet of the dead emperor.

昌西陵 嘉庆帝的孝和睿皇后之陵。此陵规模较小,无方城、明楼。但有其特色:一是隆恩殿藻井彩画为丹凤展翅;二是隆恩殿与琉璃花门之间有御河;三是宝城围墙前方后圆,可产生极佳的回音效果。此外,宝顶前嵌有一溜石板,若在第七块石板上轻唤一声,可听到响亮回音。这就是昌西陵著名的回音壁和回音石。

Western Changling It is the tomb of Empress Xiaohe Rui of Emperor Jia Qing. It is smaller than the tomb of an emperor and does not have the "Square City" and Memorial Tower. The motif on the cofferred ceiling of Long'en Hall is a phoenix instead of a dragon; a canal runs between Long'en Hall and the Glazed-Tile Gate; the wall surrounding the earth mound is square in front and circular behind. The front of the earth mound is lined with stone slabs. When one utters a sound close to the seventh slab there is a loud echo.

昌妃陵 位于昌陵与昌西陵之间，内葬嘉庆帝十二位妃嫔。

Changfeiling The mausoleum between Changling and Western Changling is the burial ground of 12 concubines of Emperor Jia Qing.

慕陵 清代第八位皇帝道光帝（1820
—1850年在位）之陵。清道光年间,政
治腐败,武备废弛,国势日衰。慕陵原
在清东陵,因地宫浸水,将耗资二百
多万两白银、历时七年建成的陵寝废
掉,另在清西陵重建。依其"规制稍从
俭约"的旨意,慕陵裁撤了圣德神功
碑、华表、石象生、方城明楼、琉璃花
门等建筑。但其建筑规制、材质结构
却精美异常,造价惊人,毫无"俭约"
之气。图为慕陵碑楼内石碑。

Muling It is the tomb of Dao Guang,
eighth emperor of the Qing Dynasty who
was on the throne between 1820 and
1850. The corrupt emperor spent 2 million taels of silver on the construction of
his tomb in the area of the Eastern Qing
Tombs. But when it was finished seven
years later, the burial chamber was
prone to groundwater. The emperor a-
bandoned it and built another one in the
cemetery of the Western Qing Tombs.
On the emperor's order "to be thrifty",
the new tomb did not have the usual Divine Merit Stele, stone ornamental
columns, "Square City" with the Memorial Tower and the Glazed-Tile Gate.
But it cost no less than any other imperial tomb. The picture shows the stone
tablet in the Stele Tower of Muling.

慕陵迎客松 慕陵龙凤门前有两棵
迎客松,主干倾斜,支干横生,枝繁叶
茂,犹如好客的主人,弯腰颔首,彬彬
有礼地迎接游客。

Greeting-Guests Pine at Muling Two
pine trees stand in front of the Dragon-
Phoenix Gate of Muling. Their trunks
bend forward and their branches stretch
out as if they were greeting guests, thus
their name. After so many years they
are still flourishing.

慕陵隆恩殿 为金丝楠木殿。不施彩画，以蜡涂烫。门窗隔扇，梁柱雀替，天花藻井遍雕云龙、蟠龙七百一十四个，龙身在云雾中翻腾舞动，气势非凡，甚为壮观。图为大殿前廊。

Long'en Hall of Muling The hall is built with precious nanmu wood. The wood is not painted. A thin wax coating shows the golden veins of the raw wood. The cofferred ceiling is carved with 714 dragons swimming amidst clouds and mist. The picture shows the front of the hall.

天花板木雕　步入隆恩大殿，金丝楠木馨香扑鼻，举目仰望天花板，但见群龙张口鼓腮，喷云吐雾，形成万龙聚会、龙口喷香之势。

Relief Carvings on Cofferred Ceiling　A nice smell of nanmu wood can be detected inside Long'en Hall of Muling. The dragons carved on the cofferred ceiling swim amidst clouds and mist. One feels the nice smell came from their breath.

Stone Archway　The stone archway at Muling serves the same purpose as the Glazed-Tile Gate of other imperial tombs as the entrance to the burial chamber. This archway is made of white marble and has four columns. The mythical animal on top of every column means to ward off evils. The inscriptions on both sides of the overhead board are in the handwriting of Emperor Xian Feng. The overhead side boards are carved with dragons and phoenixes in relief.

石阶　慕陵无方城明楼,故设三路石
阶,阶栏由汉白玉石凿就,顶级栏杆
左右伸展至宝顶围墙。整座建筑雅系
端庄,简繁得当,不落凡俗,为皇陵中
最有特色的陵寝。

Stone-Paved Flights　In place of the
usual "Square City" and Memorial Tower of other imperial tombs Muling has
three flights of stone in front of it. The
uppermost white marble balusters reach
to the wall that surrounds the earth
mound. Muling is the only one of the
Qing Tombs thus decorated.

慕东陵　原为慕陵妃园寝,因道光帝
之孝静皇后葬入才升格为皇后陵。

Eastern Muling　The tomb was built for
imperial concubines. But when Empress
Xiaojing of Emperor Dao Guang was
buried in it, its status was raised accord-
ingly.

慕陵宝顶 矗立于 2.5 米高的月台上,其外围有龙须沟环绕,上有长 1米多的铜铸出水口。宝顶三面为高大围墙,正面为三路石阶踏垛。围墙不挂灰,不涂红,磨砖对缝,干摆灌浆,墙顶覆黄琉璃瓦,墙体随地势起伏,整个建筑简洁朴实。

Earth Mound of Muling   The mound sits on a 2.5-meter-high terrace and is surrounded by a moat. Copper drainage pipes, one meter long, protrude from the wall of the moat. High walls stand on three sides of the mound. In front of the mound there are three flights of stone steps. The wall is not painted. The bricks were meticulously polished before they were used to build the wall. The wall is topped with yellow glazed tiles and rises and falls along with the terrain.

崇陵 中国封建社会最后一座皇帝陵,内葬光绪皇帝(1874－1908 年在位)及孝定景皇后。光绪皇帝三岁继位,其时清廷为慈禧太后专权,他便成为没有实权的儿皇帝,一生郁郁寡欢,无所作为,崩年三十八岁。

Chongling It is the tomb of Guang Xu who was on the throne from 1874 to 1908 and his empress Xiaoding Jing. Guang Xu ascended to the throne at three but was only a puppet because Empress Dowager Ci Xi held the actual power. He led a depressed life and died at 38. Congling is the last tomb of Qing emperors. His successor, Emperor Pu Yi, was dethroned.

崇陵隆恩殿 殿内顶梁、大柱均为桐木、铁木，素有"铜梁铁柱"之称。大殿基部还有近2米宽的斜坡"散水"，月台环绕汉白玉石雕栏，整座建筑巍峨宏阔，保存完好。大殿内部金碧辉煌，祭台前按照清皇室祖制摆放着各种复制的供品。

Long'en Hall of Chongling The beams and pillars inside Long'en Hall of Chongling are of tung wood and ironwood. The terrace is surrounded by white marble balusters. At the base of the hall a two-meter-wide slope drains rain water. The well-preserved hall keeps replicas of sacrificial objects used during the Qing Dynasty.

梓宫 崇陵地宫为四门九券,梓宫安放于金券内"宝床"上。棺椁周身朱红涂漆,雕有镀金藏文和梵文经咒以及卐字不到头的底饰纹案。隆裕皇后棺椁置于左,其顶盖上雕有金凤一只,挺立山岩,展翅欲飞,旁边云团朵朵,脚下海浪涛涛,山花灼灼。画面布局紧凑,造型优美,刀法玲珑,不失为高水平的木雕艺术品。

Burial Chamber of Chongling The burial chamber has nine vaults and four gates. The coffins are lacquered in dark red, inscribed with Buddhist scriptures in Tibetan and Sanskrit languages and decorated with chains of the symbol for longevity. The coffin of Empress Longyu on the left is carved with a picture: a phoenix stands on a huge cloud-shrouded rock; below the rock sea waves surge and wild flowers bloom. The carving displays a very high artistic level.

珍妃墓 崇妃陵西宝券内葬珍妃。珍妃是光绪皇帝的宠妃,因支持光绪帝新政被打入冷宫。1900 年,八国联军攻入北京,慈禧太后外逃前将她赐死于紫禁城内珍妃井。1901 年回京后,令人将其尸体捞出,草草葬于西直门外恩济庄。1915 年以贵妃礼葬入崇妃陵。

Tomb of Lady Zhen Lady Zhen, a favorite concubine of Emperor Guang Xu, is buried in a vault of Congfeiling. She supported the emperor's political reform and was hated by Empress Dowager Ci Xi. In 1900 the Allied Forces of Eight Powers invaded Beijing. Before she fled Ci Xi ordered Lady Zhen be drowned in a well in the Imperial Palace. When she returned to Beijing Ci Xi got Lady Zhen's body out of the well and buried her at Enjizhuang Village outside the city. In 1915 Lady Zhen was re-entombed according to the standard for an imperial consort.

崇妃陵 位于崇陵东侧1公里处。内葬光绪帝之珍、瑾二妃。地面建筑主要有东西朝房、东西班房、享殿等,均以绿琉璃瓦覆顶,规制虽较帝后陵低,却也小有规模。图为享殿。

Chongfeiling The mausoleum one kilometer to the east of Chongling keeps the remains of Lady Zhen and Lady Jin, two concubines of Emperor Guang Xu. Main buildings above ground are court halls, duty-officials rooms and the Offerings Hall. Their roofs are covered with green glazed tiles. The buildings are smaller than those at Congling. The picture shows the Offerings Hall.

行宫 清西陵行宫是专为皇家祭陵之人营建的公馆。宫门内分左、中、右三部分。左为銮舆库，是存放车轿之地；中为行宫，为帝后居住之所；右为营房，乃守卫兵将居住之处。行宫规模宏大，幽雅肃静。

Temporary Palace The Temporary Palace was built for the royal family members to stay when they came to the Western Qing Tombs. The palace is divided into three parts: the part on the left was a garage for the imperial carriages; the central part was living quarters and the part on the right were residence of the guards. The surroundings of the Temporary Palace were quiet and tranquil.

永福寺　俗称喇嘛庙,位于行宫西侧,是清朝皇家御用寺庙。清制,帝后忌辰,由喇嘛在西配殿诵经,超度亡灵,故乾隆皇帝特在西陵境内建寺,专事皇陵祭祀活动。

Yongfu Temple　The Lamaist temple to the west of the Temporary Palace served the royal family only. On the anniversaries of the death of emperors and empresses during the Qing Dynasty, lamas were sent for to chant prayers. Emperor Qian Long built this temple for the lamas to stay.

明 代 帝 陵

帝号及姓名	在位时间	陵名	埋葬地址	陪葬情况
明太祖朱元璋	1368—1398 年	孝陵	江苏南京	皇后马氏
明惠帝朱允炆	1398—1402 年			
明成祖朱棣	1402—1424 年	长陵	北京市昌平	皇后徐氏
明仁宗朱高炽	1424—1425 年	献陵	北京市昌平	皇后张氏
明宣宗朱瞻基	1425—1435 年	景陵	北京市昌平	皇后孙氏
明英宗朱祁镇	1435—1449 年 1457—1464 年	裕陵	北京市昌平	皇后钱氏、周氏
明代宗朱祁钰	1449—1456 年	景泰陵	北京市西郊金山	皇后汪氏
明宪宗朱见深	1464—1487 年	茂陵	北京市昌平	皇后纪氏、王氏、邵氏
明孝宗朱祐樘	1487—1505 年	泰陵	北京市昌平	皇后张氏
明武宗朱厚照	1505—1521 年	康陵	北京市昌平	皇后夏氏
明世宗朱厚熜	1521—1566 年	永陵	北京市昌平	皇后杜氏、陈氏、方氏
明穆宗朱载垕	1566—1572 年	昭陵	北京市昌平	皇后李氏、陈氏、李氏
明神宗朱翊钧	1572—1620 年	定陵	北京市昌平	皇后王氏、王氏
明光宗朱常洛	1620 年	庆陵	北京市昌平	皇后郭氏、王氏、刘氏
明熹宗朱由校	1620—1627 年	德陵	北京市昌平	皇后张氏
明思宗朱由检	1627—1644 年	思陵	北京市昌平	皇后周氏、贵妃田氏

清 代 帝 陵

帝号及姓名	在位时间	陵名	埋葬地址	陪葬情况
清太祖努尔哈赤	1616—1626 年	福陵	沈阳东郊	
清太宗皇太极	1626—1643 年	昭陵	沈阳北郊	
清世祖福临	1643—1661 年	孝陵	河北遵化清东陵	孝康章皇后、孝献皇后
清圣祖玄烨	1661—1722 年	景陵	河北遵化清东陵	四后,一皇贵妃
清世宗胤禛	1722—1735 年	泰陵	河北易县清西陵	孝敬宪皇后,敦肃皇贵妃
清高宗弘历	1735—1795 年	裕陵	河北遵化清东陵	二后三皇贵妃
清仁宗颙琰	1796—1820 年	昌陵	河北易县清西陵	孝淑睿皇后
清宣宗旻宁	1820—1850 年	慕陵	河北易县清西陵	孝穆成皇后,孝全成皇后
清文宗奕詝	1850—1861 年	定陵	河北遵化清东陵	孝德显皇后
清穆宗载淳	1861—1874 年	惠陵	河北遵化清东陵	孝哲毅皇后
清德宗载湉	1874—1908 年	崇陵	河北易县清西陵	孝定景皇后

Imperial Tombs of the Ming Dynasty

Posthumous Title and Name of the Emperor	Reigning Period	Name of the Tomb	Burial Place	Wives Buried with the Emperor
Tai Zu (Zhu Yuanzhang)	1368-1398	Xiaoling	Nanjing, Jiangsu Province	Empress Ma
Hui Di (Zhu Yunwen)	1398-1402			
Cheng Zu (Zhu Di)	1402-1424	Changling	Changping County, Beijing	Empress Xu
Ren Zong (Zhu Gaozhi)	1424-1425	Xianling	Changping County, Beijing	Empress Zhang
Xuan Zong (Zhu Zhanji)	1425-1435	Jingling	Changping County, Beijing	Empress Sun
Ying Zong (Zhu Qizhen)	1435-1449 1457-1464	Yuling	Changping County, Beijing	Empresses Qian and Zhou
Dai Zong (Zhu Qiyu)	1449-1456	Jingtailing	Jinshan, Beijing	Empress Wang
Xian Zong (Zhu Jianshen)	1464-1487	Maoling	Changping County, Beijing	Empresses Ji, Wang and Shao
Xiao Zong (Zhu Youtang)	1487-1505	Tailing	Changping County, Beijing	Empress Zhang
Wu Zong (Zhu Houzhao)	1505-1521	Kangling	Changping County, Beijing	Empress Xia
Shi Zong (Zhu Houcong)	1521-1566	Yongling	Changping County, Beijing	Empresses Du, Chen and Fang
Mu Zong (Zhu Zaihou)	1566-1572	Zhaoling	Changping County, Beijing	Empresses Li, Chen and Li
Shen Zong (Zhu Yijun)	1572-1620	Dingling	Changping County, Beijing	Empresses Wang and Wang
Guang Zong (Zhu Changluo)	1620	Qingling	Changping County, Beijing	Empresses Guo, Wang and Liu
Xi Zong (Zhu Youjiao)	1620-1627	Deling	Changping County, Beijing	Empress Zhang
Si Zong (Zhu Youjian)	1627-1644	Siling	Changping County, Beijing	Empress Zhou and Lady Tian

Imperial Tombs of the Qing Dynasty

Posthumous Title and Name of the Emperor	Reigning Period	Name of the Tomb	Burial Place	Wives Buried with the Emperor
Tai Zu (Nurhachi)	1616-1626	Fuling	East Suburbs of Shenyang	
Tai Zong (Huangtaiji)	1626-1643	Zhaoling	North Suburbs of Shenyang	
Shi Zu (Fulin)	1643-1661	Xiaoling	Zunhua County, Hebei Province	Empresses Xiaokang Zhang and Xiaoxian
Sheng Zu (Xuanye)	1661-1772	Jingling	Zunhua County, Hebei Province Four	Four empresses and one concubine
Shi Zong (Yinzhen)	1722-1735	Tailing	Yixian County, Hebei Province	Empress Xiaojing Xian and Lady Dunsu
Gao Zong (Hongli)	1735-1795	Yuling	Zunhua County, Hebei Province Two	Two empresses and three concubines
Ren Zong (Yongyan)	1796-1820	Changling	Yixian County, Hebei Province	Empress Xiaoshu Rui
Xuan Zong (Minning)	1820-1850	Muling	Yixian County, Hebei Province	Empresses Xiaomu Cheng and Xiaoquan Cheng
Wen Zong (Yizhu)	1850-1861	Dingling	Zunhua County, Hebei Province	Empress Xiaode Xian
Mu Zong (Zaichun)	1861-1874	Huiling	Zunhua County, Hebei Province	Empress Xiaozhe Yi
De Zong (Zaitian)	1874-1908	Congling	Yixian County, Hebei Province	Empress Xiaodingjing

编　后　记

　　中国的明清帝后陵，无论是地上地下建筑、彩绘、雕刻，还是室内装饰、陈设，内容都十分丰富，是中国五千年墓葬文化的精华。其中既有中国汉文化的优秀传统，又融会了中国北方少数民族的地方特色，几乎达到了尽善尽美的程度。明清帝后陵为我们今天研究墓葬文化提供了珍贵的实物资料，又为旅游文化增加了丰富多彩的内容。

　　但是，陵寝的建筑作为一种定式，基本大同小异，这就给我们选择图片、撰写文字、编排版式带来了困难。为了不致重复，明帝后陵我们以长陵地面建筑和定陵地宫为重点，其他各陵则简单提及；清帝后陵则以定陵为重点，详细介绍各单体建筑的名称、作用、特点，给人以清代皇陵的总体印象，其他各陵则重点介绍最有特色的部分，凡雷同的均予以删除，以方便读者阅读。

　　在本书的编辑过程中，我们得到了明十三陵管理处朱力、魏玉青，清东陵管理处于善浦、李寅，清西陵管理处尚洪英等先生以及管理处领导和专家们的鼎力相助，我们感谢之余，谨致敬意。

编　者

POSTSCRIPT

　　The buildings, paintings, sculptures and interior decoration of the imperial tombs of the Ming and Qing dynasties are the highlight of the 5,000-year-old Chinese burial history. They contain the best elements of the culture in Central China and characteristics of the Manchu nomadic tribe from Northeast China. Their design and construction are flawless. The tombs provide us with valuable materials for the study on burial customs. They have become much liked tourist attractions.

　　The design of every imperial tomb is much the same one from another. We felt difficult to avoid repetitions when we selected photos and wrote the text. We finally decided to arrange the Ming Tombs with the buildings of Changling as the main part of above-ground structures and the burial chamber of Dingling as the main part of underground structures. As for the Qing Tombs we described in particular the name, function and characteristics of various parts of Dingling so as to present a general picture of the imperial burial grounds of the Qing Dynasty.

　　We extend our thanks to Zhu Li and Wei Yuqing of the Ming Tombs Administration Department, Shan Pu and Li Yin of the Eastern Qing Tombs Administration Department and Shang Hongying of the Western Qing Tombs Administration Department for their great help in compiling this album.

Editors

编　辑：　望天星　施永南

翻　译：　刘宗仁

撰　文：　施永南　望天星
　　　　　李　寅　魏玉青

摄　影：　望天星　朱　力
　　　　　李春耕　董宗贵
　　　　　罗文发　王春树
　　　　　何炳富　胡维标
　　　　　张肇基　刘春根
　　　　　姜景余

装帧设计：　廖增宝　严　伟

图书在版编目(CIP)数据

明清帝后陵：中英文/刘宗仁译. —北京：中国世界语出版社,1995.7

ISBN 7－5052－0264－2

I. 明… II. 刘… III.①陵墓－名胜古迹－中国－明代－画册－汉、英②陵墓－名胜古迹－中国－清代－画册－汉、英 IV. B928.76－64

中国版本图书馆 CIP 数据核字(95)第 12108 号

明清帝后陵

＊

中国世界语出版社出版

北京 1201 厂印刷

中国国际图书贸易总公司(国际书店)发行

(中国北京车公庄西路 35 号)

北京邮政信箱第 399 号　邮政编码 100044

1997 年(16 开)第一版第二次印刷

ISBN 7－5052－0264－2/K·33(外)

06800

85－CE－466P